Lonely at '15

By Donna K. del Villar

DORRANCE
PUBLISHING CO
EST. 1920
PITTSBURGH, PENNSYLVANIA 15238

Dorrance Publishing Co
585 Alpha Drive
Pittsburgh, PA 15238
Visit our website at www.dorrancebookstore.com

ISBN: 979-8-88683-497-0
eISBN: 979-8-88683-585-4

Lonely at '15

A grieving widow at '87'~
Here's my life story!
Names and places are real!

I want to start by introducing my parents and their background, because, as you know, if it hadn't been for them, I wouldn't be here! My mother, Evelyn, was born on Nov 12, 1916 in Pratt, KS.. to my grandparents, Thomas and Lena Gray. Mother attended school, grades 1-12, in a one room schoolhouse, which was originally a coal house. Mother graduated from grade school, and that's when the family decided to move to long beach, California, where mother attended Wilson High School.

This is where she met her first love Van! Everything was good until 1933, the year mother and Van would graduate. The big earthquake happened, causing much destruction. My granddad, Thomas, worked at a cleaners, but after the cleaners was destroyed, he could not find work, so he decided to move the family back to Missouri to be near relatives. He got a job working on a farm.

Mother missed Van very much but as time passed, she met Clarence, who was very handsome and could play the guitar and sing. In fact, he would come to see her while driving his car with his feet on the steering wheel, playing his guitar and singing to my mother. He was the youngest from a family of twelve. He had to quit school in the ninth grade in order to help support the family. He worked very hard seven days a week to help out!

Before I go on about my parents, I want to tell you the best story yet about how my grandparents met! On February 11, 1916, Thomas L. Gray and Lena Rose Lasser were each on the train to see relatives in Pratt, Kansas. They were cordial and attracted to each other. They exchanged names and their destinations. It was night and the train stopped, Thomas said, "Lena, this is where we get off." He was twenty-one and she was twenty two at the time. After getting off the train, he said, "Lena I have a friend who lives in the house next to the train station. He will give us a ride to each of our relative's homes." She said, "Oh, that would be nice." They got to the house, the man answered the door and invited them in, and a sign inside read, "justice of the peace!" He asked them their names, then the reverend got his bible and started reciting a prayer, then he said, "Lena do you take this man to be your lawfully wedded husband?"

Lena was in shock but thought to herself, "I'm twenty-two and never even had a date, this might be my last chance." So, she said, "Yes, I do."

The reverend then said, "Thomas, do you take this woman to be your lawfully wedded wife, until death do you part?" Thomas said, "I sure do." Long story short, my mother, Evelyn Rose Gray, was born November 12, 1916, almost nine months to the day after my grandparents were married! After being told this story years later, I always thought that's how the tv show "married at first sight" originated, ha!! My granddad was 6'3" and grandmother was 5'2" with eyes of blue! Shortly after they married, granddad was called to leave for WWI in the army, but after being shot in the right hip, he was discharged. Due to his injury, he had a limp in his walk the rest of his life.

Thomas L. Gray, 6'3", Age 21 and Lena Rose Lasser, 5'2", Age 22

Thomas and Lena Gray and daughter Evelyn, 1916

Clarence and Evelyn dated until July 1934. Remember, they met in 1933. That's when one of Clarence's sisters, who lived in Ohio, wrote a letter telling him there was plenty of work to be had in Ohio! At this point, Clarence and Evelyn decided to elope and go live in Ohio without telling Evelyn's parents. Off they went! They married July 7, 1934. Clarence got a job where he would work from sunrise to sunset seven days a week. He still enjoyed playing his guitar and would also yodel and sing. He was so good people started calling him "Jimmie" after Jimmie Rodgers. The following month after they arrived in Ohio, Evelyn found out a baby was on the way.

That was me!! That's when my parents realized they had to make a better living!

In the meantime, Thomas and Lena had moved from Missouri to a place called Jarbalo Kansas. Grandad worked on a farm and grandmother got a job at the veteran's hospital in Leavenworth, Kansas. Over the years, they had managed to save a few dollars as granddad was very frugal, only allowing grandmother a quarter or fifty cents per week and never giving my mother (Evelyn) any spending money. Since she was their only child, she was expected to do and did all the housework, helped iron and do the cooking. With the money they had managed to save, they were able to purchase a place high on a hill overlooking Jarbalo. For two thousand dollars, my grandparents bought the small house on a good piece of land. They called it the mound.

Mr. and Mrs. Clarence Austin Simms

Clarence and Evelyn dated until July 1934, when they decided to elope to Ohio to be married, because his sister (Mary) told them; jobs were plentiful.

"The land of milk & honey" they were married July 7, 1934 both were dressed in white.

Clarence never had a complete education, as the youngest of 12, he had to quit school in the ninth grade to help support the family. He worked very hard every day of the week (including Sunday) to help out. My dad Clarence was a very hard worker; he would get up at 5:00 A.M. He had to walk seven miles up and back every day to his work and back home. He did not have a car because he sold it in order for him and my mother to make the trip to Ohio. It wasn't long until tragedy hit. My dad came down with the smallpox, he was unable to stand, let alone walk. Small pox is a mass of infectious, small sores, which he had all over his body.

Mother would bathe each sore two or three times a day. Because my dad was unable to work, my mother wrote her parents and asked them if it would be alright if they came to live with them! Mother wanted to be near her parents when I was born! Her parents were happy as they thought they had lost their daughter forever! They said yes, so away my parents went to Jarbalo, Kansas. When dad was well enough, he got a job milking cows! It was very hard to find work, as it was the middle of the great depression

Soon on April 10, 1935, I was born at the Cushion Hospital in Leavenworth, Kansas. When I was six months old it became obvious to my mother and dad that living with my grandparents was not going to be too good as the living quarters were very small. So mother started reading the ads in the paper, until one day she read an ad placed by a rancher in Fort Worth, Texas. He needed someone to milk his cows twice a day (thirty-six of them) and someone to bake bread and feed his twenty-two bird dogs twice a day. He was a wealthy rancher and hunter. Since dad had become very good at milking cows, they decided to take a chance and move to Texas. The job included housing, some pay, and food.

Upon arrival, everything looked good. My dad would sit on a small, three-legged wooden stool and milk the cows by hand and mother would bake bread for the bird dogs. After milking so many cows twice a day, my dad's hands at night were sore and bleeding. Mother would apply medicine and wrap them for the next day. Everything seem to be okay, but mother was still nursing me, she hung her under slip in the closet, and the next morning there was a big hole in the breast area. Some of her milk had gotten on her slip, and the rats found it.

Mother said she became very scared, as she could lay in bed at night and could hear the rats running in the walls. In the day she would sometime see one, she said they were about a foot tall, and would sit up and look at her. She was afraid they would eat me from the smell of milk. Luckily, I never encountered a rat!

While in Texas, mother became pregnant but didn't realize it until one day at two months when she lost the baby. It had not started to mature and was very small, so they buried it in a bottle. As far as they could tell it was a boy.

When I was able to walk, I would take my cup and go to the barn so my dad could squirt milk into my cup. I would drink the warm milk from the cup. I liked it because it was warm, straight from the cow! The result was that I wanted my milk warmed, until I was 5 years old.

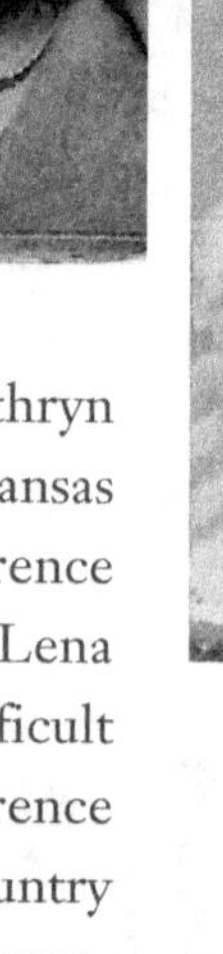

On April 10, 1935, Donna Kathryn Simms was born in Leavenworth, Kansas (which was next to Jarbalo) to Clarence and Evelyn, making Thomas and Lena proud grandparents. It was very difficult to find work, especially when Clarence could only do farm work, and the country was in the middle of "The Great Depression."

When I was close to four years old, my parents knew I would soon be ready to start school. Even though times were so tough, my parents managed to have enough money to buy a car so we could move to Kansas City, Missouri, for me to be enrolled in Kindergarten and for dad to get a better job. He had milked cows by hand for so long his ring finger was a size 13; his hands had gotten very large! They would hurt him so bad, and Mother told him, "We have to get you some relief." So, off we went to Kansas City.

Mother and dad got an apartment close to the school, and my dad was trained to be a Greyhound bus driver. My big thrill was when dad would return from a trip and mother would take me down to the bus station to bring him home in our car but first he would always let me ride in the bus while he took the bus to the Greyhound garage. I would get to sit up in the front seat by the door with him driving the bus. When he came to a railroad track he would stop the bus and open the door! I would say, "Why do you do that daddy?" and he would say, "To let the train go through." My eyes were as big as teacups looking for the train.

Mother would walk me to school then come meet me after school to walk me home. In doing so, mother met several other mothers with their children. That's when she decided to give me a birthday party. So on April 10, 1940, when I turned 5, I had all together about 20 girls and boys come to my party. Other than one girlfriend (her name was Mary Anne), that is the last time I ever remember having friends come to my house, and I was never allowed to go to anyone's house. I became very lonesome, and that is when I started building my make-believe world!

In our apartment we had one large closet. I would take my dolls and other toys in the closet and make believe they were my real live friends. Mother always made sure I had very nice clean clothes (that she made) and my hair was always curled so I always looked nice!

While I was in the closet, I would sing. One day, my dad heard me and decided I should go up to the local theater and be in the Saturday night talent show. In between movies, anyone who wanted to perform could do so! While my dad played the guitar, I would sing. The song everyone liked the most was "Playmate."

Dad was trained to be a Greyhound bus driver.

Donna- Age 3

Donna- Age 4

Donna- Age 5

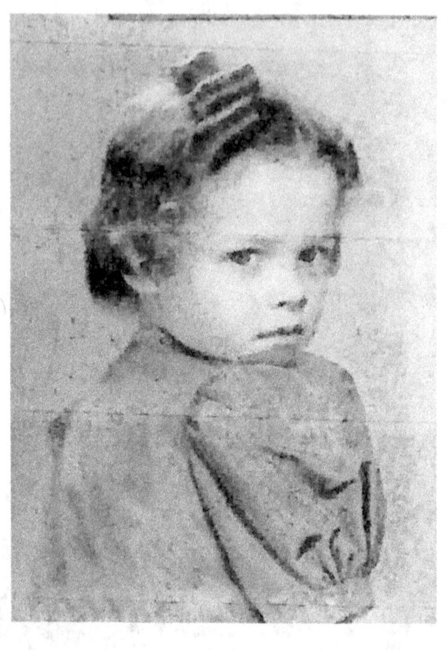

1940 - Donna was 5 when she would sing on stage while her dad played the guitar at the local movie theater on Saturdays for the talent show. The song everyone liked most was "Playmate."

1941- Since Donna was ready to start grade school, Evelyn decided to find work to help make ends meet. By now, Jimmie had become a Greyhound bus driver and loved it. Evelyn's first job was a junior typist for Encyclopedia Americana. She continued until Donna graduated grade school. All the while, Evelyn saved enough to put a down payment on a house at 2516 Jackson Avenue.

My dad loved his job as a Greyhound bus driver, but he only made $1.85 per hour. Mother got a job as a typist at the Encyclopedia Britannica, and she worked there until I graduated from grade school.

* * * * *

Getting back to my grandparents, my grandmother's parents died and left their homestead in Carrollton, Missouri to all 12 siblings. Since my grandparents had worked while living in Jarbalo, Kansas, they had saved quite a lot of money and thought it would be nice to try and buyout all the siblings. They were successful so they moved to the 60 acre wheat farm which had a barn, chicken coops, and a fairly nice but rundown house. They soon re-modeled the house and it was very nice.

Since mother and dad were both working, in the summer, mother would take me to spend the summer with Grandmother and granddad in Carrollton, MO. Even with the limp my granddad had he was still able to ride the machine to plow the ground and plant the hay but when it came time to reap the harvest he would hire 4 men to bail the hay. I would walk behind the tractor carrying a bucket of water in case any of the hired hands needed a drink of water.

I also would help grandmother cook a big lunch for the crew. Usually in the early morning we would pick out the chickens, kill and feather them, then fry up the delicious chicken. It always amazed me after we would cut the chickens head off, the body would flop around for a few minutes, (I never could figure that out.) Grandmother would go along the fence and pick blackberries so she could make a cobbler. We also would have mashed potatoes, gravy, corn on the cob, and coleslaw. Oh yes, we had homemade bread right out of the oven. Soooo good! (On the farm, lunch was the main meal.)

Because they had a lot of chickens, a certain time of the year the chickens would lose their feathers and the wind would send the feathers flying all over the yard. They had a beautiful front yard right by the road where people would drive by! There were six oak trees, so the wind would blow those leaves all over, too! On Sunday we would sit out in the front yard and watch the people drive by and wave at them.

Anyway, one day grandmother said, "It's time to clean the yard." So I got the rake and the wheelbarrow and started cleaning the yard. Everything was clean and beautiful when I got done. (It took me all morning.) I was so proud! But when I picked up the wheelbarrow handles, it tipped, and the leaves and feathers went flying all over the yard again! Oh no!!

Grandmother had a long handled shovel she picked it up, holding it high over her head. She started chasing me around the house saying, "I'm going to whip you all over these 60 acres." Luckily, after three trips running around the house, she sat down and said, "Oh, nevermind, I'm out of breath anyway." I was laughing so hard but I still ended up cleaning the yard again! I knew grandmother loved me too much, and she would never hurt me.

Another funny thing happened on their back porch. They had a wash pan that we would fill up to wash our hands when we came in from working outside. There was plastic over the window on the door so the sun wouldn't shine through and make it too hot in the house. Anyway, I washed my hands, backed up to the door, pushed on it with my back, and threw the water from the pan out the door, not knowing my granddad was sitting on the backdoor step. He wasn't too happy but again, I started laughing. As it was, I thought it was very funny.

So I could have a friend, they bought me a dog. He was a beautiful collie and I named him "Sport." Sport and I used to walk and run along the creek. I was so happy. I loved him so much. That's when I met "Larry Lightfoot" walking his dog. He lived on the next farm. One day my granddad said, "You can invite Larry for dinner". So I did, and before we ate, granddad said the prayer and he said, "The father, the son," and pointed his finger at Larry, "and the Holy Ghost." I never saw Larry again.

At home when I was eight, mother taught me how to clean the house. I had to make the bed seven times before she approved. She also taught me how to iron dad's Greyhound uniforms. All the while mother was working, she managed to save enough to put down payment on a three story house at 2516 Jackson Avenue. this was their dream home! Her idea was to rent the two top floors out. Right away, mother started going to garage sales to find furniture to furnish the second and third floor so she could rent them out.

In the meantime, my dad was having to drive the bus to a destination where he would have to stay overnight before coming back to Kansas City, Missouri. This was not good!! Dad was a very hard worker but was easily swayed so he started going to a bar before retiring for the night, drinking beers and spending his paycheck dollars. It was a while before mother found out about it. That was when the greyhound company had to fire him because he had been drinking and showed up for work drunk! Mother did not hesitate, she went to a lawyer and filed for divorce. She told me what she did, I told her if she went through with the divorce, I would not go with either one of them. (I was twelve and could make that decision.)

Grandmother's Homestead

After re-model

Lena's Chickens

Me and my dog Sport

Anyway, dad was so sorry for what he did and didn't want to lose mother and me so mother decided to give him another chance and he couldn't drink again. It was a very hard time for a while until dad was able to get a job, it was driving a big diesel tractor, a transport truck. He did this for thirty-twoyears until he retired. During this period, he was able to purchase his own tractor and lease the trailers so that gave him a much bigger paycheck!

Mother had the third floor of the house rented out so everything was going pretty well. It was my job to clean the house, iron, and prepare some meals. Because I did these things just the way mother had taught me, she decided to reward me. She bought me a teddy bear coat, which was very popular at the time but she made it very clear I was only to wear the coat on special occasions. Well, one day I decided to just leave my pajamas on while I cleaned the house (they were short summer PJs and this was winter with snow on the ground.) Everything was fine until I had to go outside to empty the garbage; the garbage can was in the ground out by the garage.

I knew how cold it was outside and I saw my teddy bear coat. I said to myself. "It will only take a minute to get out to empty the garbage," so that's what I did. I put the coat on, and away I went. Oh no!! when I came back to go in the house the door was locked. Oh boy, now what do I do!! The only thing I could think of was to go down to where mother worked to get the key. I knew I couldn't stay outside all day. I happened to have 10 cents in the pockets of my coat (that's what it took to ride the streetcar). Mother had taken me to her work before so I knew how to get there. Until my dying day I will never forget the look on mother's face when she saw me standing in the lobby with the teddy bear coat on. She gave me the key and 10 cents to get back home. When she came home I was grounded for a week. To me, that wasn't a lot of punishment because I hardly ever got to go anywhere.

1947- I graduated from grade school, and again, I went to my grandparent's farm. These trips each summer were very nice. I really enjoyed them. Grandmother had so many sayings she would tell me, and when I stop to think about all of them, I have really lived my life based on all the standards she lived by!

Here are some!!

1. Do me once but don't do me twice!
2. Goodbyes are not forever-goodbyes are not the end, they simply mean, I'll miss you until we meet again.
3. I didn't need you when I didn't know you and I don't need you now!
4. God helps those who help themselves
5. If you don't like yourself, nobody else will!
6. Cleanliness is next to godliness!
7. God does not give you what you can handle- God helps you handle what you are given!

1948- I entered East High School as a sub-freshman
1949- I became a freshman
1950- My granddad, Thomas Gray, passed away at age 55. There was no warning, he had worked on the farm until 2:00 PM. He started having pains in his heart. He was rushed to the hospital and Mother and I were able to drive down to the hospital and were standing by his bedside; we could hear a gushing sound. It was blood running into his heart. I'll never forget that sound! That was the way 1950 started out for me.

Now, I will explain the title of my story. I was a very lonely girl being an only child and literally having no friends to speak of! My mother was always very strict with me but I know my mother loved me. I was the apple of her eye! I came into puberty when I was ten, which is pretty young.

One day, while I was walking up the stairs in school between classes ,I came to the landing in the stairs and for some reason I turned and looked back. That is the first time I saw David; he was looking up at me and smiling (no one had ever looked at me that way). I smiled back and from then on, we kinda met in the halls from time to time. He was a varsity football player. One day, he asked me if I'd like to go to the football game Friday night.

It was a surprise, but my mother said I could go if she took me and picked me up after! Throughout the rest of my story, I am going to refer to David as "D." "D" was a senior and eighteen, and as time went by, we met at the school football games. He would come over to my house when mother and dad were both gone, as I knew they would not approve.

Anyway, as time passed, he was going to graduate and he wanted us to get married. Things still were not good for me at home. He said I could still go to school! It all sounded so good to me! We decided to elope! Over in the state of Kansas, you didn't have to have your parents consent to get married at age 15. We did just that, then naturally we had to tell our parents.

I had already met his parents. They liked me a lot but my mother was devastated and did not talk or have anything to do with me for two months. In the meantime, "D" graduated and got a job at the service station. As soon as he got a couple of paychecks, he got us an apartment. It was not a very nice one but now we could be together. It wasn't long until I was pregnant, so that was the end of my going back to school. It didn't take long for "D" to start staying away from time to time, leaving me alone. I knew we had made a mistake, but I was too proud and scared to tell my parents. I also knew I had to get a job. By now I was 16, as of April 10, 1951.

1951- I went to the phone company, as they would hire and train you at 16. In a couple of weeks, I became a long distance line operator. They didn't know I was pregnant, at least for a few months.

The apartment "D" had gotten for us was not furnished so he went to Pacific Finance and put money down to buy furniture, including a baby bed. After a few months , one day I came home from work and the apartment was empty except for the baby bed. "D" had not made any payments so they repossessed the furniture. By that time, my due date was very near (three months) it was winter and there was a broken window in the apt. the heat had been turned off so I climbed up in the baby bed to sleep and used my coat to keep warm. (now comes the big surprise!

I finally got up the courage to call my mother. That's when she informed me she was pregnant and due about the same time as I was. She was very nice and told me "D" and I could come live on her 2nd floor (she had furnished it to rent out but it happened to be vacant now.) Up to now, I had not seen a doctor, so she wanted me to go to her doctor. I told "D" so we went to live with my parents. A couple of months passed and on Oct 14, 1951, mother had my sister Denise. Thirty-two hours later, on Oct 15, 1951, our beautiful, perfect son Robert Lee (which was David's middle name) was born. This was Denise's nephew!! This was quite newsworthy. We had the same doctor and same hospital room and it made the front page of the K.C. Star.

While "D" and I with baby Robert were living with my parents, "D" brought our payments to Pac Finance up to date so we could get our furniture back. I found out I was pregnant again and so was my mother, wow!! This was getting out of hand. Ha!! Anyway, mother told my dad we need a bigger place so we can raise our second family. They started looking until they found the perfect place at 1700 T.C. LEA Road in Independence, Missouri. This was a one acre lot and a very nice home, too! By the way, while living in Independence, Mother got pregnant again. Oh! No! this made a total of three. All of a sudden, I had a sister, a brother, and one on the way! (I'm not the only child anymore.)

For some reason, "D" had a brilliant mind and was very knowledgeable of foreign cars. He answered an ad in the paper for a foreign car mechanic. It was in South Gate, California. He went to California and got the job. "D" got an apartment and wanted me and Bob to come out to California to live and have our new baby. Mother said she would take me, Robert, and the furniture to South Gate. She rented a U-Haul and took us! (That is how we came to be in California.) Our 2nd beautiful son Daniel was born on Oct 31, 1953.

Dick and Donna, 1950

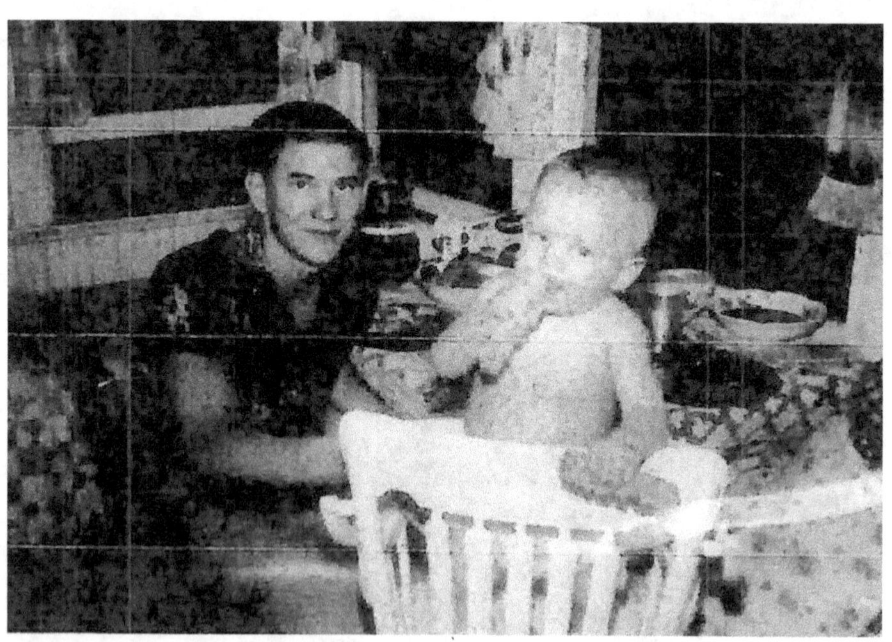

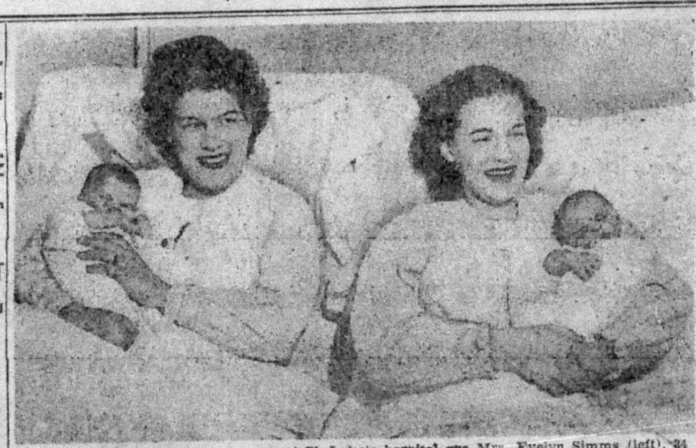

THE KANSAS

VOL. 72. NO. 31. ✶ ✶ KANSAS CITY, OCTOBER 18,

RANGE TO ROYAL

Western Air Prevails at Show as Quarter Horses Make Contest Debut.

A TITLE TO MISSOURI MARE

Animal Owned by St. Joseph Couple Is Declared Champion in Class.

NEW MARK FOR CARLOT

Iowa Firm Pays $85 a Hundred Pounds for Feeders From Colorado.

BULLETIN.

Xander's Ballerina, a black yearling owned by Mr. and Mrs. Perry McGlone, St. Joseph, Mo., was chosen champion quarter horse mare of the American Royal.

[ADDITIONAL ROYAL NEWS AND PICTURES ON PAGES 3, 8 AND 9.]

WHO'S WHO?—Sharing a room at St. Luke's hospital are Mrs. Evelyn Simms (left), 34 years old, 2516 Jackson avenue, and her daughter, Mrs. Donna Dumler (right), 16 years old, 6024 East Sixteenth street. Mrs. Simms holds her new daughter, Denise Yvonne, 5 days old, while Mrs. Dumler holds Robert Lee Dumler, 4 days old, her son, Mrs. Simms's grandson,

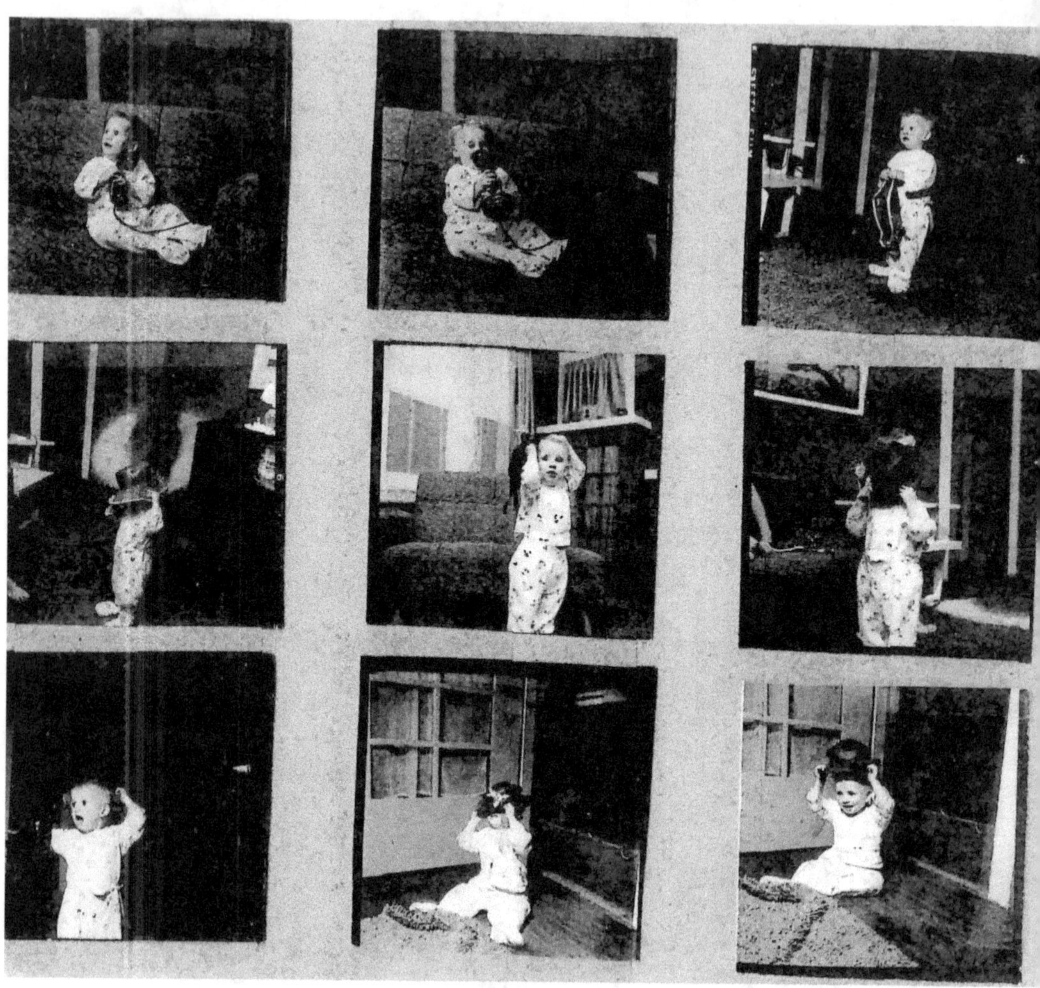

At one year old, Dan was such a cute little boy; his favorite pastime was putting on hats.

Again, D would stay out all night or away for several days from time to time. It was just me and the boys then one day this foreign car dealer in Hollywood called and said he heard about D and how good he was with foreign cars. He offered D a big increase in salary! So that's when we moved to Hollywood on Sunset Boulevard in the bungalow style house. (There were six units.)

Upon moving to Hollywood, at first everything seem to be okay until one day the owner of the place where we were living came while D was at work. He said he wanted the rent or he would evict us. Of course I did not know our rent had not been paid. He gave us two weeks to pay or get out.

By this time I had gotten to know some of the neighbors! One couple had five children, then another couple, the husband worked, but the wife June was a stay at home housewife. I knew I was up against it, somehow I had to get a job, this time. D had been gone almost a week! I knew I didn't want to call my mother, so I confided in those two couples that were my neighbors. Right away the couple with the five children offered to watch the boys and the other couple said, "You come eat your meals with us."

I tried to figure out why D was so weak that he would keep putting me and the boys in jeopardy. I knew he was adopted; I had met his adoptive parents, Faye and Ben Whipple, they seem to be very nice people. Faye was a diabetic who had to have both legs amputated. She was 20 years younger than her husband Ben! As for mental illnesses, there was no indication along that line. When D was a teenager Faye and Ben adopted another boy Paul, and as far as I knew there was not any physical abuse from them to either of the boys.

My worrying about where D was short-lived as one day there was a knock on the door! When I answered the door, two detectives let me know D had been arrested and was in the county jail on several charges (selling dope, assault, armed robbery) I was so torn. I didn't know he was doing any of these things but right then I knew I had to make myself and the boys a new life.

1954

I answered an ad for the Upjohn Company in Hollywood for an accounts receivable clerk that would train me. Remember I did not graduate from high school! I only had one bottle of milk in the refrigerator, the rent was behind again, and the landlord was going to put me and the boys out. I finally called my mother and told her everything. She wired me $50 so I could get some milk and food.

I was nineteen when I went to the interview with the DC center manager, Lyman Williams, and I told him everything. I even told him I was trainable if he would give me a chance! He said, "in that case can you start tomorrow?" I said, "oh yes," and that was October 19, 1954. Bob (Robert) was three and Dan was one.

Right away the neighbors did what they said they would do for me. I had to ride the bus to work. (I used some of the money mother had sent me to buy a weekly bus ticket. The day I went to work the landlord came by at night and told me, "now that you have a job, I am going to garnish your wages so I can get my rent." I didn't know what to do because in those days if your wages got garnished then you lost your job!

The next day when I went to work I asked to see my manager (Mr. Williams). I told him what was going to happen (I will never forget it). He stood up from his desk chair he said, "How much do you owe?" I said $285, he reached down in his pocket pulled out some bills and counted out $285. He said, "Here you don't owe any rent, and no one can bother your wages! You can pay it back at $10 or five dollars per week." I really couldn't afford to pay my rent until I had earned a few week's pay. I still didn't know what I was going to do word got around work and I could not believe the kindness I received.

One person gave me a ride to and from work, and several others would bring care packages to my home. I was so embarrassed but also so thankful! After a few months I had saved some money to keep my rent paid up but my ultimate goal was to get my boys where they could stay in their own home and not have to depend on the neighbors. It was becoming obvious to me that even though "Bea" was such a nice person to watch the boys, she really couldn't spend much time with them because she had five of her own.

Anyway one day I decided to look in the paper at the babysitting ads and lo and behold there was this ad, 65-year-old lady will babysit as a live in for room and board five days a week. I couldn't believe it but I called her she said she would have her daughter-in-law bring her out to meet me and the boys. Her name was Helen, and she had a slight shuffle in her walk but she seemed to be nice and liked the boys! Helen came to live with us during the week and her son would come get her to spend the weekend with them!

Remember my mother had brought the furniture that D had bought for us while in Missouri from Pacific Finance! Well guess what? D had not made any payments to them since we moved to California. The company transferred the past due balance account to Pacific Finance in Burbank, California. Well one night Helen and I were at home with the boys and the doorbell rang. It was this guy named Hank- a collector from Pacific Finance.

I told him the situation (by that time D was out of jail) but I had not seen him. The only way I knew he was out of jail and living nearby was his mother Faye told me. I only had an idea where he might be. I told Hank I could pay the money owed at one dollar per week if that was okay. He said he would have to let his boss know and see what they could do.

Anyway I learned this a few years later! Hank went back to his office in Burbank and told his boss(who is Ben del Villar) you have got to see this woman; she has two adorable boys and she is so nice and cool. A couple of nights later the doorbell rang again and the man said, "I am Ben del Villar from Pacific Finance." I invited him in and he gave me a payment book so I could pay one dollar per week. He wanted to know if I knew where D was. I told him I thought I did and it was only a few blocks away. He said, "Would you like to show me?" "I'll take you there and bring you back," I let Helen know I would be back in just a little while.

I was impressed because Ben had a dark blue suit, white shirt, and tie on, and he was so polite to me. He opened the car door for me (no one had ever done that before) but we were unable to locate D so Ben took me back home. I told Ben as soon as I got enough money I was going to file for divorce. I started sending my payments of one dollar a week. This is what Ben told me several years later! (Now, it was two years later.) I had not seen or talked to Ben. Helen was still with me!

1956

Ben was at work one night. He was looking through his address book and he called a couple of girls to see if they were available for a date on Saturday night! Each one already had plans so he took another look at his book and saw my name. He said to himself, "I wonder if she ever got a divorce?" Helen was still with me one night when the phone rang. I picked the phone up and said hi Ben! (I'll never know why I said that but I did). Ben said he about fell out of his chair; remember this was two years since I had seen or talked to Ben.

"How in the world would I say that?" he said ."I was wondering how you are doing and did you ever get a divorce?" I said, "We are okay, no I haven't gotten the divorce but as soon as I can afford it, I will." Ben said, "Well I was wondering if you might go to a football game at the Colosseum Friday night with me , my sister Van, and her husband Bob." I said, "I don't feel I should because I'm still married. He said, "I understand but maybe you can think about it and I'll call you back in a couple of days." When I hung up the phone, I told Helen what Ben had said. She said, "You go, you need to go," so when Ben called back, I told him I could go but I'd have to meet him at the end of the driveway so the neighbors could not see me because I didn't feel right with them knowing I was still married. Ben said, "That's fine whatever makes you feel comfortable."

On Friday night I met Ben and he took me to his mother's house (which was where he was living and it was two blocks from the Colosseum so we could walk to the game. Van and Bob were already there so he introduced me to them and his mother. It was fun to be with Ben and go to the game. When he took me home he said, "I was so proud to take you with me tonight" he leaned over and kissed me and I could feel my heart jumping and I kissed him back and soon the rest would be history.

Again, I had him let me out of the car at the end of the driveway! After that I decided to let my neighbors know what had happened. They thought it was wonderful! From then on Ben would call or come over two or three times a week. I could tell the boys really liked Ben and he would play and hug them. At work I had been promoted to accounts receivable assistant CR manager for over 7000 accounts with doctors and hospitals in California and Arizona.

One day one of my employees told me there was a two bedroom duplex for rent where she lived (her name was Rosemary Csepke). I had been thinking of trying to find a place closer to work and close to a school as Bob was ready to start school (kindergarten) soon. It was within walking distance from my work so one day on my lunch break Rosemary took me over and showed the duplex to me. I could walk to work, put Bob in school, and Dan could be in the childcare program. Rent was only $65 per month. This meant I would not need Helen anymore because I could take the boys in the morning before work and get them on my way home (the walking was good exercise) and that was in high heels; if I tried that today it would probably kill me!

I was 19 when I first met Ben and when I started work at Upjohn

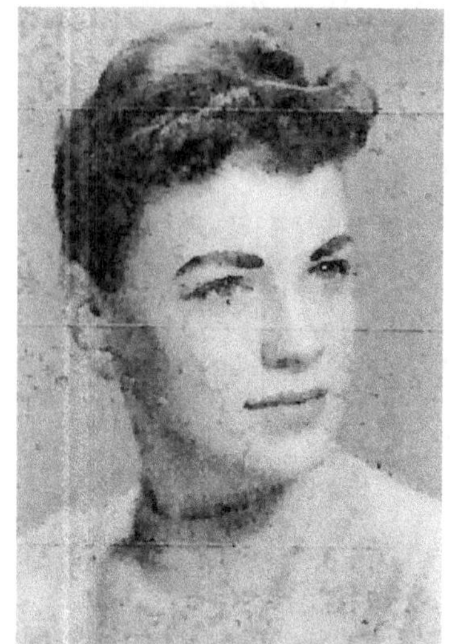

Bob 3, Dan 1

In 1950, Donna was a young adult when she left home to get married. The marriage did not work but produced two fine boys, Robert, 10-15-51 and Daniel 10-31-53. Donna had moved to Hollywood, California where she met the love of her life, Ben del Villar. They married in 1957, and Ben (who loved the boys) immediately adopted them as his own.

Donna, 22

Bob, 6 and Dan, 4

Again, I told my boss Lyman Williams, and he said, "Here is $65 for your first month's rent we will just add it to what you owe." (I was about to be able to pay the first loan off!) I thanked him for the kind favor. Another employee named Vivian McKean had a husband in the army stationed at Camp Pendleton ,California. He was gone during the week but came home on the weekends. The Saturday I was going to move Vivian and her husband Ken showed up at my front door and said we are here to move you (they had a trailer). I was shocked, but very thankful that I had help to move. Ben came with a trailer too, so altogether we were able to move me and the boys in one day. (Goodbye Sunset Boulevard!)

It was hard to say goodbye to the neighbors who had helped me so many times but they were glad to see me take the step forward! Rosemary was so kind, she would watch the boys if Ben and I wanted to go out.

Getting back to Ben, there was no question we had fallen in love! He told me in his family it was a tradition whenever the sons would date the next morning they would ask their mother, "Well what did you think?" When Ben asked her about me, she held up her hand and pointed her finger at him and with her Spanish accent she said, "This is the one." He said, "but mama she is married, getting a divorce, separated, has two sons and she is not Catholic." Again his mother pointed her finger and said, "This is the one." I could never figure this out as I had only met her one time for about fifteen minutes.

Just before I met Ben in 1954, he had been married for a short time to a girl he met in college, and they had a son Ben Junior who was born in 1952. His ex's name was Pat, and they divorced soon after the baby came! Finally, I was able to see a lawyer Bob Winckler he was able to start divorce proceedings for me.

With this starting to take place, one day Ben said to me, "I've dated several women. Some very beautiful and smart, athletic, good cooks, good dancers, caring, but you're all those rolled into one. I love and respect you so much. I would be honored if you would spend the rest of your life as my beautiful wife." (At the time D was back in LA County jail), Ben said, "I want to adopt the boys so they can carry my name. I loved them the first time I saw them."

Ben knew a wholesale jeweler in LA. He took me down there so I could pick out a diamond for the ring Ben wanted to get for me so when the divorce was final he could put a ring on my finger. This was funny when the jeweler brought out a tray of diamonds I looked at them they were very small to large. I took my finger over the whole tray and said, "I'll take that one!" It was the last one on the tray and the biggest one (half carat). Ben said, "I knew she had good taste, so how much is that one?" The jeweler said $285 (that just happened to be exactly what Ben had in his pocket so he gave the jeweler cash and said this has to last a long time." (Today the ring is worth $3000) He gave me my engagement ring on Easter Sunday 1957. I'm still wearing it 65 years later!

Ben Jr.

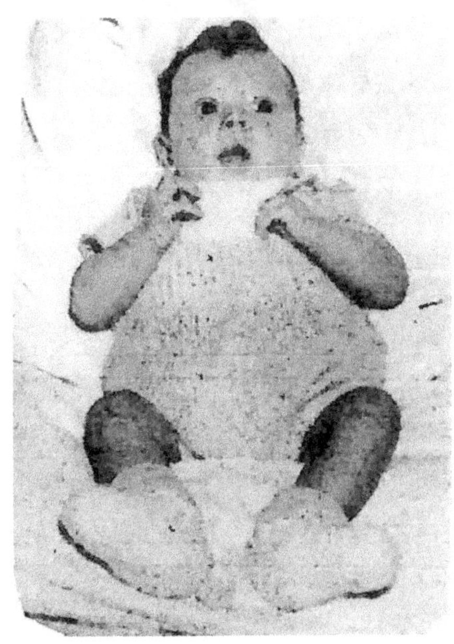

Born Mar 24, 1952

15 months, June 1953

20 ms Nov 1953

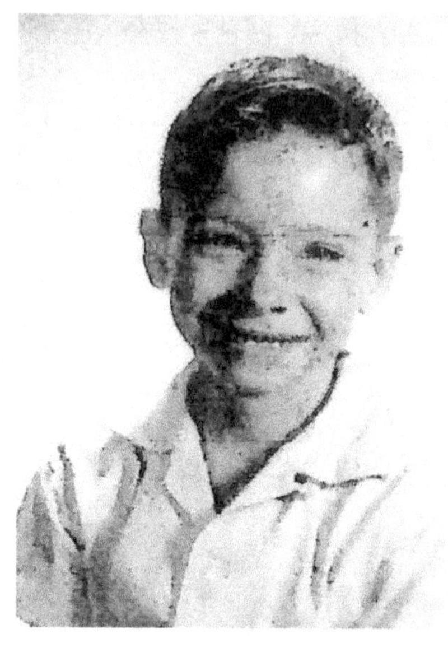

May 1959

Ben del Villar Jr.

While Ben Sr. was in college his first year, he met and eloped with Patricia Wright in 1951. They had a son, Ben del Villar Jr., born on Mar 24, 1952. By 1954, the marriage was over. After completing his college courses at UCLA, he received a degree in finance. He went to work for Pacific Finance as a collector then manager of the Burbank, California office.

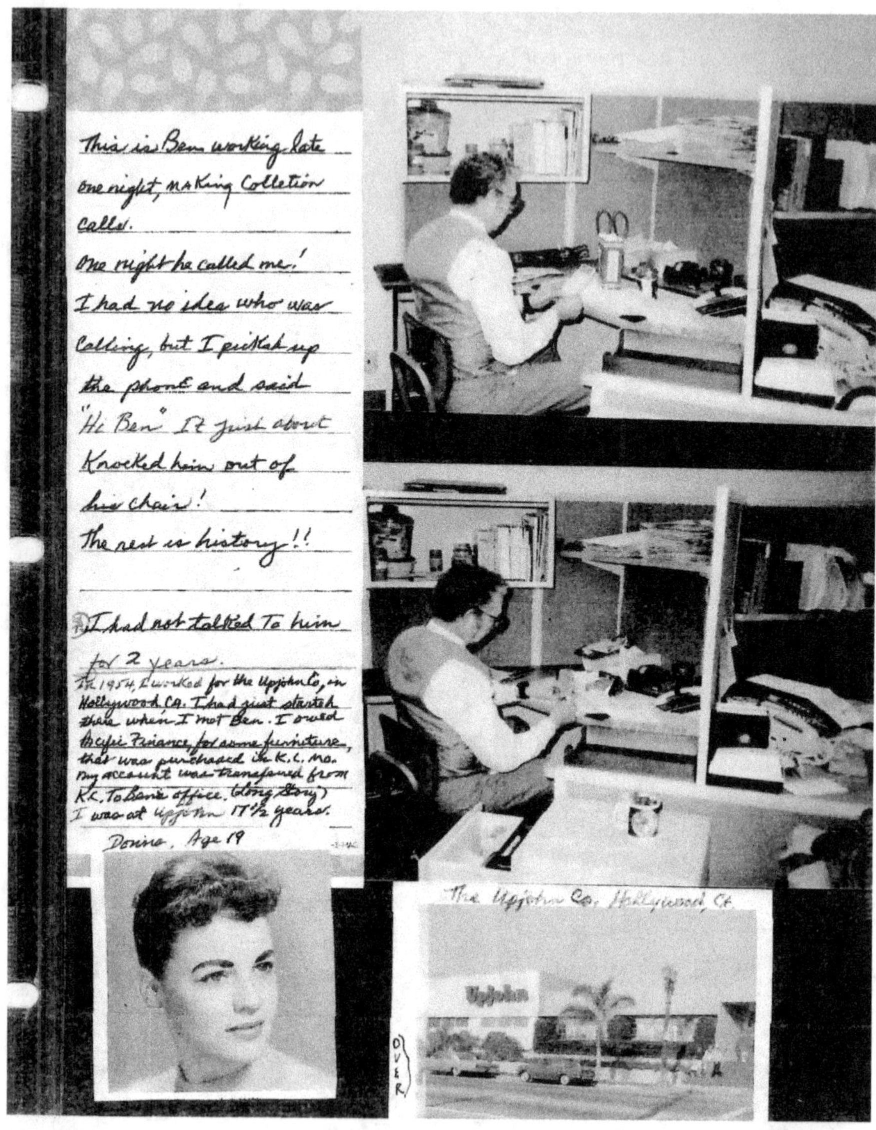
This is Ben working late
one night, making Collection
calls.
One night he called me.'
I had no idea who was
Calling, but I picked up
the phone and said
"Hi Ben" It just about
Knocked him out of
his chair!
The rest is history!!

I had not talked To him
for 2 years.
In 1954, I worked for the Upjohn Co, in
Hollywood, CA. I had just started
there when I met Ben. I owed
Pacific Finance, for some furniture,
that was purchased in K.C. Mo.
my account was transfered from
K.C. To Ben's office. (long story)
I was at Upjohn 17 1/2 years.
Donna, Age 19
The Upjohn Co, Hollywood Ct
Upjohn
OVER

Bob, 6 and Dan, 4

Ben and Donna married May 25, 1957, at ages 29 and 22

The lawyer went down to the county jail to see D and he got D to sign the divorce papers and sign the boys over so Ben could adopt them. (D was going to be transferred to Folsom prison in California). Everything was final, and we all went to court including the boys!

Ben and I were married May 25, 1957, at the Little Brown Church in North Hollywood! Van and Bob kept the boys while Ben and I went to Palm Springs for our weekend honeymoon. We would later be married in the Catholic Church (another story, later.) Ben moved into the duplex, 5927 Willoughby, where the boys and I had been living of course it became much smaller but I didn't mind I was so happy to know how much Ben and I loved each other and the boys had a dad who could give them the good family life they deserved.

Right away, Ben made out a budget so we could start saving to get a down payment to buy a home. After he figured the budget, he would get five dollars per week. He had to buy gas for the car) and I got two dollars of course I still owed some dollars at Upjohn so I paid one dollar each week out of my two dollars until it was paid off. Ben even figured in dollars for a vacation with the boys each year.

During my job at Upjohn, I needed to hire someone and I did. Her name was Rue McClanahan and she was upfront and told me she needed a job so she could pay her way to New York because someday she would be an actress. I appreciated her honesty and hired her. After a couple of years she told me she was ready to leave. I'm sure you have heard of the Golden Girls, well, one of them was Rue.

1960

Finally, Ben said, "Okay, it's time we get our own home." From the time we got married Ben and I decided we would not tell the boys about their name being changed and their adoption until they were old enough to understand. From the start when we got married, we would have Ben Junior come over and spend weekends with us so the boys could get to know each other and then someday they could call each other brother. Now, Bob was nine and Dan was seven.

1961

We found a home, a three-bedroom at 15468 Victory BLVD, Van Nuys California. Bob was ready for junior high and Dan was still in grade school but right away we knew we needed someone available to be home when the boys came home from school so they would get their homework done and not feel they were alone as Ben and I were both working. We thought it was a good idea we contacted Helen she was elated and sure enough she came to live with us during the week then with her family on the weekends. She was a blessing she kept the boys on their toes. She made sure they got to school on time, did their homework, and gave us a daily report.

Ben was determined for the boys to become active in sports also Bob joined the Boy Scouts, Dan was a cub scout, and I became a den mother. Ben signed them up for Little League. Bob was a natural; he was the boy that could play any position. Dan was very good as an outfielder he had a very strong throwing arm. Ben Junior was also in sports he was very active in high jumps and running track. (Ben took the boys and signed them up for Little League.) It kept us busy going to all the games. Eventually Ben became president of the Central Valley LL and I was the snack bar coordinator. We became very good friends with some of the parents. Because we all had something in common (our boys), we enjoyed getting together for social gatherings.

Ben enjoyed being active in sports, too! He became a certified umpire and referee. He also took up scuba diving and became a certified diver. He continued umpiring for forty years- story later! For some funny reason we started calling each other "Ma" and "Pa."

We had this one couple who we would invite over to play cards. This one night we had Jim and Diane Perkins over to play the card game "Pitch." I was sitting, waiting for my turn to bid. I was so excited I had the perfect hand to beat them all. Anyway Ben said. "It's your turn 'Ma.'" Diane said, "Why do you call her 'Ma'; it sounds so old, and she is so young and beautiful." Ben said, "Oh okay, Donna it's your turn." I was so startled I said PASS!! I looked at Ben and said, "Don't you ever call me that again," and he never did, I was always "Ma!"

1962

In Ben's job at Pacific Finance, he was having to spend more and more time at the office plus he was always under a lot of pressure to lend the money out then keep the payments coming in, even having to work a lot of weekends. He was unhappy and said to me, "Ma, I think I'm going to see if I can find another job where I can make more money and have better hours then I can be home with you and the boys more." I said, "Whatever you decide is okay with me!"

Since I had never been baptized and neither had D, our marriage was recognized by the Catholic Church as a Pagan Marriage. Because of this, that's why Ben and I could not be married in the Catholic Church to begin with. Ben told me he would like the boys to go to church and become Catholic. (They had not been baptized either.) Also, Ben said he would like me to join them. I decided since I was never baptized I wanted to be Catholic, too. Then someday we would all be united in the same religion. Ben had always been very true to his church! His 1st marriage was only a civil one too! Bob, Dan, and I were baptized in St. Elizabeth church, on June 15, 1962. Now Ben said, "The next big step is for me to write Rome, to get permission so we can be married in God's church."

1963

Finally we received our letter one year later from Rome, with blessings to re-do our vows and get married in the Catholic Church. So, in Sept 1963 Ben and I got married in St. Joseph Church by Father White. Again we went to Palm Springs to renew whatever went on the 1st time (oh my). Ben started looking in the paper and answered an ad for a company called Walter Heller and this was for a loan officer. The company was for high commercial loans.

1963

Again, through D's mother, we found out D had been transferred from Folsom prison and was doing hard time in San Quentin and would not get out until he was 69 years old. One day a letter came addressed to Bob from D in San Quentin. Bob was not home when the mail came but then when Bob came home Ben gave him the letter and said, "This is from your father." Bob never even blinked his eye; he took the letter over and dropped it in the waste basket and said. "He's not my father, you are my father!" We never knew what the letter said!

Ben got the job but it was close to downtown LA (since we had moved to Van Nuys, I had been riding the bus to my work in Hollywood). Now, Ben could take me on his way to work and pick me up on the way back home, that was a good thing as we only had the one car. Everything seemed really good!

Ben made the first loan ever to Bob's Big Boy. The amusement park called Ocean Park in Long Beach went bankrupt, the company was in chapter 11, Walter Heller Co. was ready to write their loan off. Ben said, "Wait, let me see what I can do!" Ben was able to sell all the amusement park rides and equipment to a place back east under terms that company-buying the place would pay for all the moving expenses. After that, the Walter Heller powers that be were very happy with Ben. He received a large bonus in pay. That's when we could now afford a bigger, nicer home so again we started looking (Bob was 12 and Dan was 10). Bob was ready to start high school at Cleveland High and Dan Jr. High at John Sutter Jr. High.

We saw an ad in the Sunday paper for these homes being built on one acre lots. Ben said ,"Let's go Ma!" again, I said "Okay." This was a three bedroom. Ben said, "Ma we can have a pool so the boys can swim and have their friends over and maybe Ben Jr. would like to come live with us?" I said that would be great but Ben Jr. was too devoted to his mother and rightfully so. Besides he had a girlfriend and her name was Suzy.

We had become very good friends with the credit manager at Upjohn, Gene Troup, his wife Betty, and their three children. They had a boat and would go to Lake Mead for camping and water skiing each year. They would invite us to go with them for a week each summer. So we planned to take a week off each summer and go with them; it was so much fun! I was the only one who never learned to water ski. I was afraid of the water!

Ben said, "Ma how would you like someday for us to get a boat?" I told him that sounded great! Also, in the winter Ben took me and the boys to Mammoth Mountain and taught us all how to snow ski, the boys were very good. I didn't do too bad. I only had to be brought down the hill once in a ski patrol basket when I fell on the slope, twisted my leg, and couldn't get up!

Now we were ready to sell our house in Van Nuys, as our new home at 19931 Ingomar Canoga Park was ready for us to move into. We were so excited; we knew it would be a few more years before we could have a pool put in, plus Ben said, "Ma we can have a badminton court, too?" I said, "Okay, we better start saving our pennies."

1965

When we moved in our new home, our family and friends gave us a house-warming party. It was so nice; they all chipped in and gave us a money tree! Soon our backyard was complete and we were able to get our first boat! We still only had one car but now we had to get a bigger one so we could pull the boat. (Our lake trips continued until the year 2000, by this time we were on our third boat. Our lake trip stories comes later!)

1967

When Ben and I got married in 1957, my mother and dad were unable to come to California for our wedding. Remember they had another family to raise. Finally, my siblings were old enough they could be left with family while my parents came to California for a visit to meet Ben and get to know their grandsons. The question was, what could we do to entertain them? Ben said, "Why don't we take them to the town hall party? Because your dad likes country music so much."

The town hall party was a TV show every Saturday night, featuring Porter Wagoner and Dolly Parton. Ben really wasn't too excited because cowboy was really not his style. Anyway, we drove to Long Beach to go to the show. Every time the TV camera would swing around in Ben's direction, he would scoot down in his chair so hopefully no one would see him on camera.

He was making a sacrifice just being there, ha!! Before we left to come home, Ben was slapping his leg and keeping time with the music. He was hooked- ha!! To carry this even further, after my parents went back home, one of my cousins (from my grandmother's family), her husband and their four daughters had moved to Pumpkin Center (right next to Bakersfield California). Their names were Ray and Ruby Waters. Ray had taken a job as a cattle ranch foreman; they started inviting us up for weekend visits.

Before you know it Ben was learning to castrate, dehorn, and vaccinate the cattle. He even wanted to buy some cowboy boots and a tailored suit for his work. He was hooked, Ray asked him if he would like to take some time off from work to go on a cattle drive to take the cattle up the mountains so they could graze on the grass in the Meadows. Ben was so excited he told Ray yes he would really like to go! The Cowboys started calling Ben, "the city dude."

The following weekend we went up to see Ruby and Ray so Ben could go on the cattle drive. Ray gave Ben one of his daughters saddles to ride the horse up the mountain all the way up the mountain Ben could see the Cowboys legs were straight into the stirrups but his were high almost to his waist because the horse would take four steps going up the hill Ben's shirt pockets started rubbing on his breasts and in his pants with each step was rubbing on his cheeks (butt) he couldn't figure it out by the time they reached the top of the mountain there was a cabin that the Cowboys would stay overnight after they got to the cabin one of the Cowboys started to cook their dinner.

He opened a can of beans and cut his finger. He said, "Does anybody have a Band-Aid?" Another cowboy said, "I do." Ben, said "I'll take four, right away." Ben put one on each breast and one on each cheek. One of the Cowboys said, "When you get home your wife is going to think you were up here with a bunch of women." They all laughed but Ray said, "Oh I'm sorry I forgot to adjust the saddle for you, that was my youngest daughter Linda's saddle." Anyway, at that point Ben was a bona fide cowboy, till the end of his life. (He loved cowboy music and movies, too.)

1968

One day Bob came home and told Ben and me that there was this groovy-looking girl in his Spanish class, her name is Kerry Corcoran, and he was a friend of her brother Brian as Bob and him were on the basketball team! Bob said, "Brian and I want to double date Saturday night to go to the movies."

Ben said, "You want to take Brian to the movies?" "No," Bob said, "It's his sister Kerry! Before that, Bob had never seemed interested in girls; he was so much into sports. Ben said, "Sure son, but you know the rules, you treat her with respect!" (Bob never did learn Spanish!) Ben Junior was still dating Suzy and was running track at Sierra high school. Dan was attending at Notre Dame High School playing football and setting his goal to become a physical therapist someday!

1969

Bob graduated high school and enrolled at Pierce College. He was kind of thinking along the lines of being an architect; however, after one year Bob said, Dad and Mom, I don't want you to waste any more of your money. I'm not cut out to go to college; all I want to do is work in the trades to be an electrician like my uncles are and I want to marry Kerry and have a family."

Ben said, "Well son, I appreciate your honesty; being an electrician is a good trade but in order to get married you should be able to buy her a ring pay for a honeymoon and get a car and an apartment." Bob said, "Okay, Dad, I can do that." He started going to trade school and got a job as a manager of the Gemco gas station.

Kerry Corcoran was one of eight children. Several of them were in the Walt Disney movies (the way that happened was her father was a security guard at the MGM studios.) Walt Disney was trying to cast a girl to be in the movie "Angels in the Outfield." They were having trouble finding the right person. The producer asked Kerry's dad if he had any children. He said "I sure do," and he brought Donna for an interview and they picked her, then Kevin was in several movies like "Swiss Family Robinson" and "Old Yeller" to name a few. Brian was in "Daniel Boone" then Noreen was picked to be the niece on "Bachelor Father" on TV, which ran for several years.

1970

Ben's mother was visiting at our home when she had a stroke. She was then put in a rest home near Ben's oldest brother Del's home in Garden Grove California. She passed on April 15, 1970. She was a very sweet lady and was missed by all. She was buried in Whittler, California (until then as Ben's father had requested no one in the family knew where the father was buried except the oldest son Del. Ben's father died at age 49.)

Beside the passing of Ben's mother, we had another concerning thing happen. The company

The was taken from a del Villar family history album Ben printed and albums were given to each family member in 2012.

Ben was working for (Walter Heller) decided to move their company to Orange California. Now Ben had at least one and a half hour long drive to and from work (if the traffic was not too heavy) Ben was not able to take me to work! So again, I got a ride with Kay Carpenter Dorner. She is one of the best friends I have ever had and still is!

Because it was such a distance for Ben to drive and traffic was so bad, Ben said, "Ma, I think I should try to look for another job closer to where we live." Dan would be graduating from Notre Dame High School in 1971 so that would be the best time if we did have to move. (Boy did we!)

Ben making the drive to Orange California every day. It was a chore but he tried to endure the task until the day before Thanksgiving. He left the office early (2:30) it was raining and the traffic was the worst because of the holidays, also he had to detour because of the Hollywood Christmas parade. It was 8:30 PM when he walked into our home. That was the straw that broke the camel's back!

The next day, Ben contacted the executive workforce agent. He was told, "If you can move to Las Vegas, Nevada, I have the perfect job for you." Ben said to me, "Ma what do you think?" I replied "what have we got to lose just our home, my job, oh well why not!" Then, he called the agent and told him if the job is still available after the holidays, he would like to go on an interview. Bob had done most everything his dad had told him he should do to get married. He gave Kerry an engagement ring and they set a date for their wedding!

1971

The agent said the job is still available, but they were just trying to find the right person. Ben said, "Set me up for January third!" Ben went for the interview; it was in Beverly Hills. It was with Kirk Kerkorian, the billionaire who had just built the International hotel in Las Vegas. He wanted someone to make gambling a legal debt because he was losing millions of dollars. The gamblers were brought into the hotel on junkets and would borrow from the hotel to gamble then leave and never pay it back. Mr. Kerkorian said he was very interested in Ben's background and would like to send Ben to Las Vegas for a week to see if Ben would be interested! Ben came home and said, "Ma what should I do?" I said, "go ahead make the trip for a week see what you think then whatever you decide is okay with me." Ben took a week off from Walter Heller and left for Las Vegas. After the week was over Ben came home and said, "Ma I think we should go for it." Okay, Las Vegas here we come! The timing was right because Dan could register at UNLV to continue his education. Kerkorian said he would put Ben up at one of the bungalows in back of the Flamingo hotel which he owned too! Ben had told him I was working and we had a house to sell then had to find another home in Las Vegas plus one of our sons was going to get married in June.

After we had decided to do all this guess what? One February morning, the Slymar earthquake happened. It was very strong and tore down most of our five foot block wall in the backyard and did some damage to our house. Ben and Dan had to leave for Las Vegas. Dan would stay with Ben in the bungalow so he could attend school then they drove back home to Canoga Park each weekend.

I had tried to give my notice at Upjohn to let them know. After the house was sold and our son got married I would be moving to Las Vegas; now it was up to me to get all the damage to our home repaired! Plus all of a sudden, I had to learn to drive. Oh, no!! We bought a small used car, and away I went, "watch out people!" The bungalow was free rent, which really helped; however, later Ben found out that the bungalow he and Dan were staying in was the one the gangster Bugsy Seigal used to stay in when he was in Vegas.

It became a real challenge but somehow we made it through everything. Again, Ben was getting a nice increase in his salary, and because of this, Ben said, "Ma, now you can retire." Bob and Kerry were married June 12; the reception was in our backyard. One of the guests was Annette Francello!

The next big event- not only did Bob and Kerry get married but so did Ben Jr. and Suzy on August 21 and all of a sudden we had two beautiful daughter-in-laws! One weekend I went to Las Vegas, so we could look for a house to buy, as we had a buyer for our house in Canoga Park. On that weekend we did find a three bedroom home at 1557 Cherokee Lane right in back of the Boulevard Mall and across from the Ruby Thomas School.

Bob and Kerry got an apartment in Reseda, California. Bob was still the gas station manager at Gemco while in the apprentice program at night to become an electrician and Kerry got a job at Gemco as the snack bar coordinator.

Bob and Kerry del Villar - June 12, 1971

Ben Jr. and Suzy del Villar - August 21, 1971

Donna   Ben Sr.   Pat   Suzy   Ben Jr.   Kerry   Bob   Dan

Ben Jr.   Ben Sr.   Bob   Dan
A handsome foursome!

Ben collected millions from the gamblers, even some estates! The corp manager at the International said, "How do you do it?" Ben said, "I just put on my Jack Webb coat, and they say 'where do I pay'?" all our friends in Canoga Park always said he looked like Jack Webb! (on Dragnet)

1972 this was our 1st home in Las Vegas

Our new car Ford Fairlane! I'll tell you about it later
when we get to the cars, boats, and motorcycles.

After marriage Ben and Suzy moved to Colorado so Ben could attend Colorado State College to pursue his education to become a forestry engineer. I ended up being at the Upjohn company 17 ½ years. Anyway we got moved. Dan was going to school in the day and got a job taking care of a very wealthy man, who was disabled and needed 24 hour care. Dan was able to study while on the job! I started decorating the house. Ben would tell all our family and friends to come see us; the bar is always open! They did and we had a lot of company and it was a lot of fun.

Ben really liked his job; he did go to court and made gambling a legal debt then he started collecting from people who had left Las Vegas owing money. He was really making an impression throughout the hotel casino industry. Different hotel managers would ask Ben "how do you do it? He'd say "I just put on my Jack Webb overcoat and they say where do I pay?" some of our friends would say Ben looked like Jack Webb on Dragnet!

After I had decorated the house I would find myself looking for things to do as I had always been a busy person. I asked Ben if he cared if I volunteered at the Sunrise Hospital (which was walking distance from our house) and he said, "Not at all, whatever makes you happy." Because of Ben's status at the International Hotel he was allowed many free perks (like going to see a show). We went to see "Elvis" three times, oh boy he was the best! They're could never be anyone that could replace him, ever. The volunteering was very rewarding but just didn't seem to keep me as busy as I would like o be!

1972

Finally one day I looked in the want ads and saw an ad placed by Vegas Village Dept Store and supermarket they wanted someone for 2 days per week, as paymaster, (will train) long story short, I got the job then after several months the girl I was relieving was quitting the company. They asked me if I would work full time! I said I would have to check with my husband and let them know. Ben said, "Ma if it makes you happy go for it." Vegas Village had 11 stores with 300 employees. Their home office was in Salt Lake City Utah. I took the job and was there 6 years that's when I said, "If I'm going to work full time I need to find another job where I can make more pay." (this took place in 1978!)

1973

We did a lot of entertaining; Ben and I were both working and Dan was going to school and now had a job as a security guard at night at the Aladdin Hotel. At the end of 1973 our world fell apart. Kirk Kerkorian sold the International hotel and the Flamingo to the Hilton Corp with the stipulation that Hilton would keep all the management. Well that didn't happen. He let them all go! Including Ben! So Ben was looking for another job but was having no luck.

Everyone in the other hotels said he was too qualified and would not hire him for the kind of pay he was used to so again Ben said, "Ma I'm going to try my luck as a car salesman, I've never done anything like that before but I'm going to try!" Ben did get a job with the Mazda car dealer in Las Vegas. Anyway, Ben was a natural.

He sold more cars in the first month than anyone else. This went on for 6 months until one day the president of the Flamingo Hotel called Ben and said, "We need a top notch collection manager and I know you would be the one if you're interested." Ben said, "I'll be there Monday morning." Come to find out, Ben was the only one from the International Management that was ever re-hired by Hilton! This was an answer to our prayer!! One of the things involved Ben going on trips to collect from the people that owed money from the gamblers junket flights flown in by the hotel. He took me to Miami with him on one of his trips.

Ben in his office at the Flamingo Hotel and Casino

Ben and Donna at the Hotel Miami Beach Florida

1974

One day Ben said, "I've got a honey." I replied, "You got a honey? When did you get a honey?" He said, "One day I was walking in back of Wal-Mart, I looked in the dumpster and there she was." I said, "If you knew then what you know now, maybe you should have left her there." He said, "No way, then I would not have all these good meals you make for me."

In 1957, when we married ,Ben had a 1950 motorcycle. One day, he said, "Ma is it okay with you if I buy a newer motorcycle, a Harley? "I said, "A Harley, that means you can take me with you!" "Oh yes, that's what I want to do, so you and I can see this country." Again, my reply was, "If that's the case then yes!" He said, "You're so good to me and this time we will pay cash." So Ultra Glide Harley two seater here we come! We joined the Harley H.O.G. group and became bonified Harley owners group members; all together through the years we went cross country three times, went through all but five states in the US. Our biggest delight was Bob and Kerry gave us our first beautiful granddaughter on July 2, 1974. They named her Erin Kathleen.

1975

Ben Jr. graduated from Colorado State with a degree in Forest Management Science and we all went to his graduation in Ft. Collins, Colorado. (We were all very proud.) Ben Jr. went on to do his graduate studies at Oregon State. After graduating he was employed by the Forestry Service and moved to Shafter, California and Suzy became a timekeeper for the Forest Service.

Ben and I went on a lot of trips on the motorcycle; also we still went to the lake for a week in the summer. The count was thirty-two people (friends and family); we always had a great time, and so did everyone else! This was the year we started having the del Villar family reunion and this was continued every year except for 2020 and 2021 were cancelled because of the Covid-19 pandemic. 2019 was our 44th reunion.

1976

Bob and Kerry gave us another beautiful granddaughter born March 16th and they named her Colleen Francis. Grandmother Gray passed away September 13th . I still miss her! She would always tell me I was an optimist because I would write uphill!

1977

On May 17, 1977, Ben and Suzy gave us a granddaughter and they named her Amy Kathleen (now we have three beautiful granddaughters.)

1978

I decided if I was going to work full time, I should try and find a job where I could make a better salary. Again I found an ad in the paper for administrative assistant at a new distribution center to open in Henderson Nevada for Levi Strauss & Company, a company with training at their main home office in San Francisco. Long story short, I was hired they sent me to San Francisco for two weeks training, and my job would include supervisor for payroll, accounts payable, purchasing, mailroom, inventory, and archive records. (whew!! Not bad for a non-high school graduate.)

1974
From left to right
Evelyn (mother)
Kerry (daughter in law)
Erin (Granddaughter #1)
Donna (me)
Grandmother Gray

This was our five generations picture

1975 del Villar
1st family reunion

Ben's mama and her (12) children

1978

This turned out to be a really big year for us! My dad retired and their second family had grown, married, and had families. My parents decided they wanted to move to Nevada so they could be close to Ben and me as we were the oldest and would have the wherewithal to care for them if needed in their golden years.

Ben said, "Ma we need to find a bigger place to park a boat, then we can go to the lake whenever we want." I agreed as where we were living the traffic was becoming very busy! We found homes being built off Tropicana in back of Liberace Plaza. You guessed it! We put a deposit on 1694 Valley Glen Court, Las Vegas, three-bedroom, half acre lot.

Another beautiful grand baby girl from Bob and Kerry born on November 22, 1978; they named her Sara Ann (that's 3)

Every time Ben Senior would see the boys he'd say, "make babies." Well, on January 31 Ben and Suzy had another beautiful girl they named her Nichol Amanda; we were so thrilled! One day (just kidding) Ben Senior said, "Don't you guys know how to make outside plumbing?" "Granddaddy" is what they all learned to call him and I am grandmother. He loved all his babies so much!

Bob and Kerry decided they wanted to move to Las Vegas, Bob would transfer unions. They wanted to be near Ben and I so the girls would get to know their grandparents. After moving they bought a home in Las Vegas, not far from us! Ben Junior was promoted and transferred to New Mexico where he was in charge of the National Forest in Albuquerque, New Mexico.

1979

Getting back to our son Dan, he was in Salt Lake City, Utah going to school. One day he called and said, "Mom and dad I met this girl her name is Nadine Deach but she goes by Deena she is going to nursing school. I'd like to bring her down for the weekend so you could meet her." This was a big surprise to Ben and me but we were glad he wanted to bring her to meet us. She was a very pretty girl. Dan and her seemed to care a lot for each other.

1980

Dan had changed his mind about becoming a physical therapist and wanted to leave school but because he didn't want to leave Salt Lake City, he decided to get a job so he could stay there. He applied and got a job as manager at JB's restaurant! You could have knocked Ben and I over when Dan told us

| Dan | Deena | Donna | Ben Sr. |

what he had done. (He had never cooked anything in his life) We could not believe it! Anyway, guess what?

Dan received an award for having the cleanest restaurant, the best sales ever! Now came the big news, him and Deena wanted to get married! Her parents lived in Mountain View, California. But Dan and Deena wanted to get married in Las Vegas; they would still live in Utah until Deena finished nursing school. Lois and Jim, , her parents arranged for them to be married at Saint Viator Catholic Church with the reception at Sam's Town Hotel Banquet Hall.

On February 16, 1980, we had a lovely new daughter-in-law. It was soon after they moved to Las Vegas. Now get this, Dan decided he would start a pest control business. (Can you figure that one out?) We couldn't! Deena became a nurse at UMC until she was ready to have their first child.

1981

On July 8, our next beautiful granddaughter was born. They named her Louisa Kathryn (my middle name) now, instead of staying in an apartment, Dan and Deena wanted to purchase a home. (Which they did!) We were blessed again when Bob and Kerry had their fourth beautiful daughter and named her Emilee Marie! This made us a total of seven granddaughters, wow! Ben would say, "I love all my granddaughters and you too ma!" Finally our back yard was finished the grandbabies loved to come over and they all learn to swim. Ben would play songs for them on our player piano. He was in seventh heaven when his grandbabies were with him!

My dad's health started to decline. He was diagnosed with bladder cancer. This changed everything. Because dad was not able to repair or do things around the house, Ben, even though he had worked in an office most of his adult life, believe it or not, he was very handy at fixing things. He could read directions very well and mother called him "Mr. Fix It" Ben didn't mind doing anything if it would help them. Mother and Dad both became very fond of Ben.

Feb 16, 1980 - Donna and Ben Sr.

Ben would say "I love all my beautiful grandbabies!" And you, too! Ma

1982

This was the year Ben and I celebrated our 25th anniversary.

Early in 1982, Bob had a sad situation. He belonged to the electrical union in Las Vegas. The job he was on closed down so he had to go to the union hall every week to sign the book so he could be sent out on another job. Some of the leaders there were not fair; they would let their friends go out before Bob. Bob said, "I have my wife and four girls I have to keep working." Still nothing happened so one day Bob decided to go out on a job anyway instead of some guys that were put before him unfairly!

At that point, the bosses threatened him and his family. Bob feared something might happen to his wife and his girls so he called the company he used to work for in California. (They had told him if he ever wanted to come back they would be happy to have him back.) So Bob took off for California. He stayed with some friends (Bob and Jenny) and drove back-and-forth every weekend for over a year. That means during this time, Kerry had to manage the girls by herself, get ready to sell their house in Las Vegas, and look for one back in California. It was a very heavy burden on the whole family. Bless her heart, Kerry was a trooper. Finally, they found a place to buy at 27558 Caraway Ln. in Saugus, California and moved.

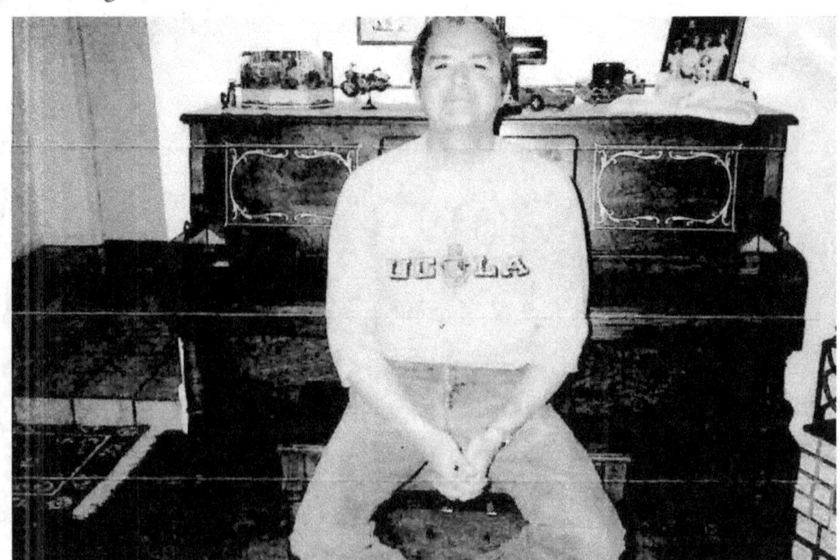

*Granddaddy missed four of his babies so he would put on his
UCLA sweatshirt and try to console himself.*

1983

Blessed again with our eighth granddaughter, born on January 13 to Dan and Deena, was Elena Marie. She was so tiny and beautiful! This is the year Dan decided to start a pest control business! He was very successful and built his accounts up to where it was very prosperous and even had several hotels on the strip and in Laughlin, Nevada. After eight years, he sold the company (that was in 1991). He was our wonder boy (wonder what he would do next). Oh my!

1983

This was the year Ben and I made our trip to Rome so Ben could carry out his father's final wishes. Ben's father passed away at the age of forty-nine leaving his mother with eleven children and one on the way. Ben's family history is another great story. (Everything was told about his family in an album that Ben and I made and gave to each family member at Christmas in 2012.) Anyway on his deathbed he told his wife Maria to bring his oldest and youngest son to him. Ben was four! To Nabor, the oldest, he said, "You're now the man of the house; no more schooling, you must find work to keep the family fed and you shall find time for yourself and maintain respect, honesty, and discipline, I have taught you then." To his wife he said, "I will be leaving you soon," for his youngest son, Benjamin, he said it will be his responsibility to complete his education through college, he will look after and share with his brothers and sisters, and most important he will go to Rome and secure the papal blessings for the next seven generations for the family. He also said to Nabor, "No one is to know where I am buried until your mother passes and can join me." Nabor kept his promise and Ben and my trip to Rome was a special holy year. Our trip to Rome is in another special album Ben's special request was made to and granted by Pope John Paul II at 11:30 A.M. October 5, 1983.

At the age of thirteen, Ben went to help his mother in a leather shop (this is where Ben learned to sew and make leather jackets). One day Ben's mother told Ben what his father said Ben was to do. Ben said, "Why me why do I have to do all that?" His mother said, "because your father said so!" That is why throughout our married life Ben would always be there to help any of his brothers or sisters when they needed help. I would be right there to help him, too.

Ben was not only a caring son, husband, and father but he was always there for his siblings. Just to name one time, Eva and her husband Edwin moved to Las Vegas in 1985. He passed away 1987 she became ill in 1997 with Alzheimer's and that's when we made sure we found a very nice assisted living place. Ben would go every week to trim her fingernails and toenails. I would take her to the doctor when necessary. Ben never hesitated to help the family.

1984

My dad lost his fight with bladder cancer. He passed at age seventy-one on March 2. At the end Ben would go over to the hospital and shave my dad's face.. Tears would run down my dad's face then he would thank Ben for the shave! Mother, Ben, and I were there at the hospital, when his doctor said, "Clarence it's a bad situation, I'm afraid we have done all we can." My dad said, "You mean there's no chance I'm going to make it? Oh I thought so it hurts so bad. Well Ma, Donna, and all the rest of my wonderful family. I guess it's my time to go, I hate it but there is nothing I can do about it! I just wanted so bad to be here for July 7th, for a celebration with my wonderful woman (it would have been their 50th) because she's tops no doubt about it.I just love all my family, children, the very breath they breathe." (that was the end.)

Mother said, "I am very proud of him and the way he reacted to the very sad news." After a year mother made a new life for herself. She joined the senior center and a group called the "kitchen kut ups." They would go to different senior centers and play music (it was a band and she played the kazoo.) She became a volunteer at the Boulder City Hospital.She had some lady friends that she traveled abroad and enjoyed herself, as she knew her time would not be far away! Mother would call Mr. Fixit pretty often ha! Oh yes, on May 3rd our precious #9 granddaughter Mary Bernadette was born to Dan and Deena (now we had enough for a baseball team).

1985

When I was growing up, around the holidays my grandmother would take me downtown Kansas City to see the department store windows decorated then we would go to the Christmas parade. I always loved the parade. I told Ben this so he made arrangements to take me on Thanksgiving to the Macy's Thanksgiving Day parade in New York. It was one of my life dreams! We stayed at the Hilton (our room was taken care of as one of Ben's perks and we had mother stay with one of her friends so she wouldn't be alone. Well she fell and broke a toe! Oh my!!

Horst Dziura

September 23, 1983

Mr. Ben del Villar
Casino Collections Manager
Flamingo Hilton and Tower

Dear Ben:

Since you are the only one left from the "old regime," your stamina, good nature and good sense speak well for you. I only know that we definitely need you to assist us in our collections, and of course, are proud to have you on our staff.

I would like to congratulate you on your birthday, and would also like to invite you and Mrs. del Villar to be my guests on an evening of your choice in either our Beef Barron Room or Peking Market, and would be happy to set up those arrangements for you.

Thank you for being such an outstanding employee.

Sincerely,

FLAMINGO HILTON AND TOWER

Horst Dziura
Vice President and General Manager

went to dinner 10/07/83

HD:mlm

MANAGING DIRECTOR
FLAMINGO HILTON
(702) 733-3111

VICE PRESIDENT
HILTON HOTELS CORP.
AND GAMING DIVISION

Pope John Paul IV–Oct 5, 1983

Ben and Donna in Rome 1983

1986

This is the year Ben and I decided to start a family tradition! Our oldest granddaughter, Erin would become twelve. We would bring them on the plane (if they didn't live by us) they would come for one week. We would take pictures throughout the week then give them a photo album when they left to go home. We would take them on a trip of their choice (snow skiing, site seeing, let them go shopping or pick an outfit they liked), then take them to a fine restaurant so they could practice their manners and learn to enjoy fine dining. We enjoyed being with the girls one on one. It was a special time for each girl and of course us!

1987

Ben was reading the Sunday paper; he saw a full page ad for new homes being built in Henderson! Ben said, "Ma look at this, you want to go look?" I could tell he wanted to go again, so I said, "Why not?" Off we went! Guess what? Ben said they were on big lots! We can have our pool and he can have his putting green. This was in Belcourt Estates. Sooo here we go again! The plans they showed us were everything we could ever want. This time we wouldn't have to wait. We could start putting everything in the back yard as soon as the house was built. We sold our home on Valley Glen (after 9 years) for a very good profit! Then bought our home at 426 Wedgewood Dr. Henderson.

1988

We enjoyed out beautiful home, family, friends, lake trips, motorcycle rides, you name it! Ben celebrated 15 years at the Flamingo! This is funny. One day Ben came home from work and said "You're lucky I came home today." I said, "Why am I lucky?" He said, "today one of the cocktail waitresses ask me if I was married. I said 'I'm so married that every time I unzip an alarm goes off' and I never saw her again." Ben was always so funny with his one liners!

Hi-Lite
ADMINISTRATIVE SUPPORT

There are several areas included in the Administrativ Support Department...they include the Mailroon Purchasing and Accounting/Payroll.

In the Mailroom, we have three great gals who work together...Eunice Fitzpatrick and Betty Smith are the mail clerks. They are responsible for mailing invoices, salesmen's reports, as well as sending and receiving reports and memos from Home Office and other sources. In addition, they work very closely with our Customer Service Department in helping them to process their paperwork. The third member of the team is Dee-Dee Lucero. She has the title of Forms Equipment Operator. She is mainly responsible for separating the OFT tags, picking tickets, invoices, replenishments, packing slips, SMO tags and other forms and reports which we all utilize each day. These items must be ready for use before 7 a.m. each day, which requires Dee-Dee to start her day at 4:30 a.m. She also does the micro-fische for CSR, Inventory and Home Office. When her time permits, she then assists Betty and Eunice with stuffing envelopes or wherever she may be needed.

As the Purchasing Coordinator, Jean Potter is busy each day taking and placing orders from various departments for such things as poly, cartons, as well as the office supplies which we use so much of. She works closely with the managers, helping to keep the records they need on hand to show last date ordered as well as shopping for the best prices and quality to stay within their budgets.

The third area is Accounting/Payroll. Jean Mellon is the Accounts Payable Coordinator. Jean is in charge of processing all of our bills for merchandise, equipment and supplies which we have ordered. In addition, she is also in charge of the petty cash and trying to keep up with the demand for change for the vending machines. Irma Murphy is the Payroll Coordinator. She processes time cards, all payroll reports and, of course, the all-important payroll checks for the employees.

Donna del Villar is the Supervisor for all of these departments. She, too, has her hands full just running from room to room keeping track of where the girls are. Donna has been with Levi since our opening in 1978. She has worked in the Accounting/Payroll Department, and then in CSR, as the Supervisor there. Now she has returned to Accounting and the multi-faceted territory of Administrative Support.

Levi Strauss Co.
Henderson NV

Donna del Villar

1986 Thanksgiving Dinner with family at our home

Dan and Deena's girls

Louisa, 5, and Elena, 3, loved for Granddaddy to play the player piano and sing to them and he loved having them with him.

You can see the slot machine in the background. When the girls all got older they got to play the machine and whatever they won, they could keep!

6-17-87

Dear Donna & Ben —
This card is just
a small means of
telling you how
much you are ap-
preciated by all
that know you. —
and to personally
thank you for all the
things that I've failed
to thank you for. —
and to let you know
how much you are
loved by

Thank you
for your kindness,
It was so good of you
May you be blessed
with happiness
For the thoughtful things
you do.

your "mother".

THE STATE OF NEVADA

EXECUTIVE CHAMBER

Carson City, Nevada 89710

RICHARD H. BRYAN
Governor

July 14, 1988

TELEPHONE
(702) 885-5670

Ben del Villar
Casino Credit Person
Flamingo Hilton
3555 South Las Vegas Blvd.
Las Vegas, NV 89109

Dear Mr. del Villar:

I recently learned that you have received a 15-year award for service from the Flamingo Hilton and wanted to extend my congratulations and best wishes for continued success.

It must be very satisfying to know your outstanding performance and dedication to your profession is recognized and appreciated. You can be justly proud of this honor.

Again, my congratulations.

Sincerely,

RICHARD H. BRYAN
Governor

RHB:kec

1989

We ended up with a most beautiful home with a 20x42 pool, casita, built in waterfall, electric BBQ, boat slab with a 23 ft boat, and Bob even put in a light pole in the backyard. Ben got his three hole putting green. We were very happy; we seemed to be busy all the time. Ben had taken up playing handball. He would usually go on his lunch break, shower then go back to work.

1990

This year we had the family reunion at our home! Mother was still enjoying her life; she would go once a year back to Missouri to see all her 2nd family. In March, Ben Sr. and Dan (father and son) made their 4th degree with the Knights of Columbus. On Father's Day Dan, Deena, the girls, mother, Ben, and I all went (took the boat) and spent the day at Lake Mead, and later on Sept 24. we all went again to the lake and celebrated Ben's 62nd birthday.

1991

Ben and I celebrated our 34th Anniversary. Ben wrote a poem to me. He was very gifted in writing poems, among other things!

1992

After eight years in the pest control business, Dan went to work for the Knights of Columbus Insurance Co. (which is a Catholic organization). Again, he was very successful. The 1st year he was in the million dollar club. He won cruises for himself and Deena. He was winning all kinds of prizes. In fact the company had to quit giving the prizes because he was winning all of them. One day Ben said to Dan, "Son, what do you do, carry a gun?" Dan said, "No dad just like you, I go into the people's home and they say where do I sign?" Later, Dan became general agent for the state of Arizona, until he retired in 2019. One thing about Dan, he has a lot of charisma, and never forgets anyone's name.

1993

The girls were always ready to spend the day with Granddaddy and grandmother.

1994

After twenty-five years at the Flamingo, Ben retired! He made our grand-daughter Louisa, who was turning fifteen, a dress to wear when we took her to the play "Nutcracker's Suite" and the dress was exactly like the one in the play.

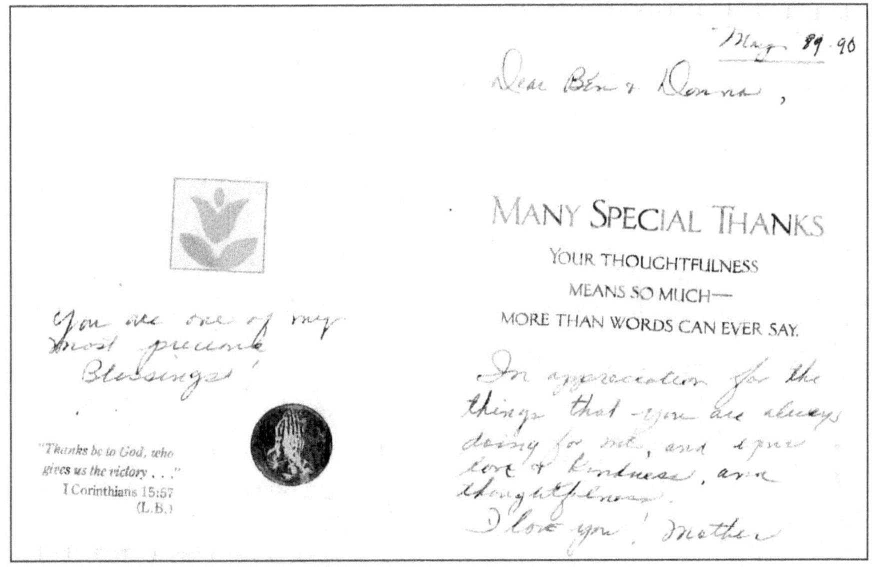

Anniversary Thoughts

May 25, 1991

Ben use to write me
beautiful poems!
This was our 34th Ann

Our strongest thoughts and feelings are most often held within
I want to let you know of mine, but how should I begin?
A young and restless business man the first time that we met,
I hardly gave it any thought, I'd seen you once and yet,
the wide eyed of innocence, an image not compared
To any girl I'd ever known, or who's company I'd shared.
There was a special fragrance just being in your presence,
the atmosphere around you was most comfortable, in essence,
there were so many feelings of comfort, joy and pleasure,
how could I know I'd say the vows allowing me to treasure
a companionship, so close and warm once you became my wife.
I slowly learned the values that would ever change my life;
you taught me how to talk things out when problems would unfold,
convincing how much more we had, than a small bank balance showed.
We built our future only by your gentle guiding hand.
with patience, love and perseverance we advanced further than I planned.
providing for our children, staying close to church and God.
I saw the progress we had made, due to your gentle prod.
Helping others when we had little, a trait you often showed
gave the warmest inter feelings, and the pride within me glowed.
As time went on our sons grew up, each can be viewed with pride,
they never strayed beyond our reach, as buried deep inside,
you instilled a set of values by example, and in your teaching,
unknown to them, though miles away your influence is reaching.
You've shown too many qualities to list in verse; However,
the ones I've known and heard about will be with me forever.
The years we've shared are many, although who's keeping score?
This heart will not be sated 'til I've had that many more

Yours Always
Ben

Ben used. to write me beautiful poems! This was our 34th anniversary

1992- Our granddaughter Mary received her 1st communion. Dan, Jim, Deach (Deena's dad), Deena, Louisa, and Mary, "Nice little family"

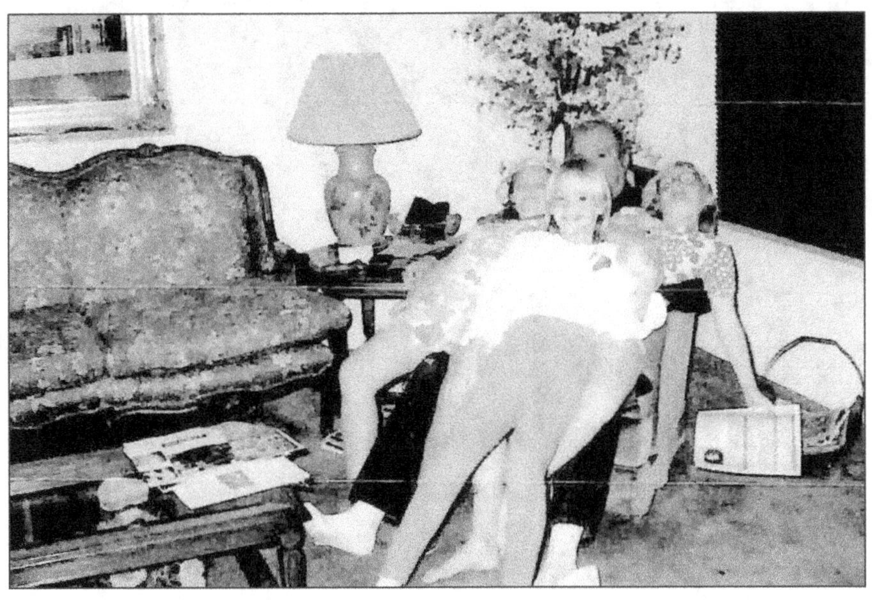

It's been a long day. Grandaddy, Louisa, Elena, and Mary

FLAMINGO HILTON

March 8, 1994

Mr. Ben L. Del Villar
426 Wedgewood Drive
Henderson, Nevada 89014-3784

Dear Ben:

For so many years, you have been a loyal employee of the
Flamingo Hilton. Now it is time to be a loyal master to
yourself.

I wish you only the best and a very healthy and happy
retirement.

If there is ever anything I can do for you here at the
Flamingo, please do not hesitate to call on me.

Sincerely,

FLAMINGO HILTON LAS VEGAS

Horst Dziura
President

HD:cj

After 25 years with the Flamingo, Ben retired.

From L to R: Sara, Bob, Kerry, Emilee, Colleen, Erin

From L to R: Amy, Suzy, Nicki, Ben Jr.

Dan, Deena, and family

From L to R: Dan, Deena, Mary, Louisa, and Elena

1994

Remember when Ben's father died, he told him all the things that the youngest would be expected to do some day. Well, when Ben was thirteen, he would go to the leather shop with his mother. She taught him how to make leather jackets. That's when she laid it on him, what his father had said Ben was to do! Ben said, "Why do I have to do all these things?" His mother said, "Because your father said so!" Anyway, Ben became quite a seamstress.

Our granddaughter Louisa was turning fifteen and she was very impressed with the musical "Nutcracker Suite" so granddaddy said we would take her to the play for her birthday. She was so excited. He asked her if she would like him to make a dress for her and she could wear it to the play! Oh she thought that would be wonderful. So they went to the library and got the book so Ben could see how the dress was made. He went to work on it. Set the table up in the family room and made her a dress just like the picture!

Picture in the library book

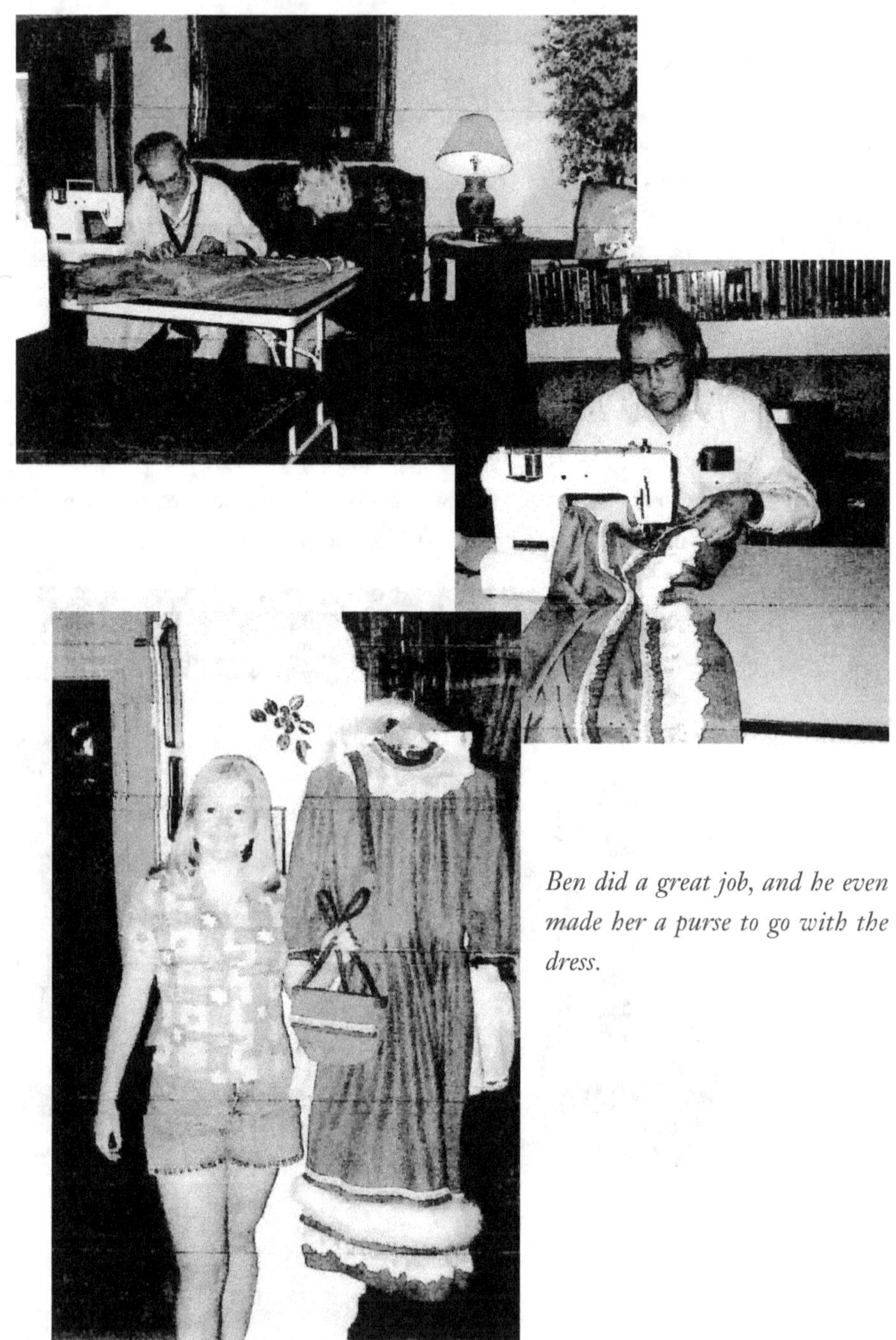

Ben did a great job, and he even made her a purse to go with the dress.

1995

Right and left we were going to our granddaughter's high school graduations! Our granddaughter Amy gave us our 1st great grandson, Alan! (this was a big 1st, a boy!!!!) After all was said and done, neither Ben nor I would trade any of our 9, beautiful granddaughters!

Almost every day, Ben would say to me, "Okay, Ma, it's your turn to retire." Finally on Dec 1st I decided he was right! I had spent 17 ½ years at the Upjohn Company, 6 years at Vegas Village, and now 17 years with Levi Strauss; this was 40 ½ years (time to go!)

1996

In January, Ben Jr's mother Pat passed away. She left them her home in Big Bear, California. In August, we hosted a party to celebrate Ben and Suzy's 25th anniversary! Then came November, Ben and I went on our 1st cruise (what a disaster, a funny one, this story is in an album).

We got our first great grandson Alan Michael! Ben used to ask the boys after they were married and were having all girls, "Don't any of you guys know how to make outside plumbing?" He could not have been happier with his 9 granddaughters and the boys knew it!

1997

Mother's health had gone downhill to the point she was unable to maintain her home. Ben and I were going out to her home in Boulder City two or three times a week. This is when we all decided to have a garage sale, plus sell mother's home, she called "the Simm's ranch" and brought her to live with us.

1998

We gave mother our front bedroom and decorated it with some of her favorite things from her home. Mother settled in really nicely. She started calling Ben (doctor) and me (nurse). Some of her friends would come see her. Ben's and my life took a change, our life now was to make hers the best we could. From that point Ben and I never left mother alone, if we couldn't take her with us we didn't go! Until later when we felt she could be alone for a few days.

1999

On March 2nd, Amy gave us our 2nd great grandson Joshua (another blessing). Some friends of ours, Whitey and Jean Mellon, had a place in Bull-head City, Arizona they were going to sell. Because we had gone down there in the past and spent many weekends playing dominos with them, we thought maybe we could take mother (it was only 93 miles) just to get away for a week-end. Well that's what we did, and we bought their place! It was two lots with a two bedroom mobile home on one lot.

Mother seemed to be doing much better and was very comfortable in her room but then all of a sudden she never wanted to go anywhere. She knew how to work the microwave and she could use the restroom without any help. She was able to watch her tv programs. She said, "You can both go down to Bullhead, I'll be fine; if I need to I'll call you." So we decided we would go for the weekend. I had put all her meals out on the kitchen counter in order by day. Well, we decided we would go and leave her there!

When we came home from the weekend, the meals were still on the counter just the way I left them, nothing had been touched. I hurried into her room, she looked so scared and said, "Where were you? I kept calling but you didn't answer." Mother had this real worried look on her face and said, "Wasn't

Our 1st great-grandson

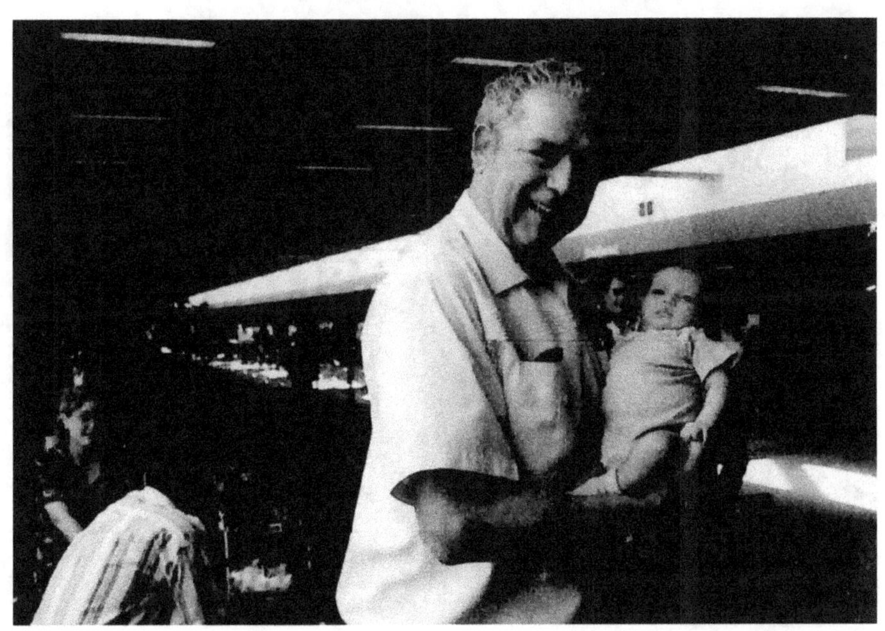

Alan Michael

Ben Jr.

I supposed to go to school today?" I said, "No mother, it's okay you already graduated." Ben and I felt so bad that we had left her!

At that point, we could never leave her again. Alzheimer's was setting in and she would hallucinate. Ben would help her with her shower and I would take her meals on a tray to her room every day. Ben and I started going to church separately and we never went anywhere together from that time on.

Ben did the 5K walk (2 ½ miles) and the high jump and won a few medals for his age group.

And the winner is

Ben Jr. was always very active in track and Ben Sr. was very proud of Ben Jr. and the two of them were active together.

2000

I already told you about Eva (Ben's sister) the doctors let us know she did not have much time left so that's when Ben and I decided we would bring her to live with us until the end. So in bedroom number two, we put Eva; we had a hospital bed. I would feed her until one day she spit out her food and she wouldn't eat for eight days and was in a comatose state until one day I was in her room and Ben came to the door of the bedroom. I said, "There's your brother Ben; he is such a brat." Eva opened her eyes, sat up, and said, "he certainly is." Then she laid back down. She was in and out until Jan 24, 2001. Ben and I were on duty 24-7. From 2001-2002, Mother held her own but her health declined until her final day Feb 16, 2003 (Dan and Deena's anniversary) On 5-29-2002, D passed away.

2003

These were mother's final wishes; she wanted to be buried in Carollton, Missouri by her parents and my dad. She had said any of the family that wanted to attend, she would pay for their transportation, lodging, and food. Again Ben wrote a poem for her. Mother passed at age 86.

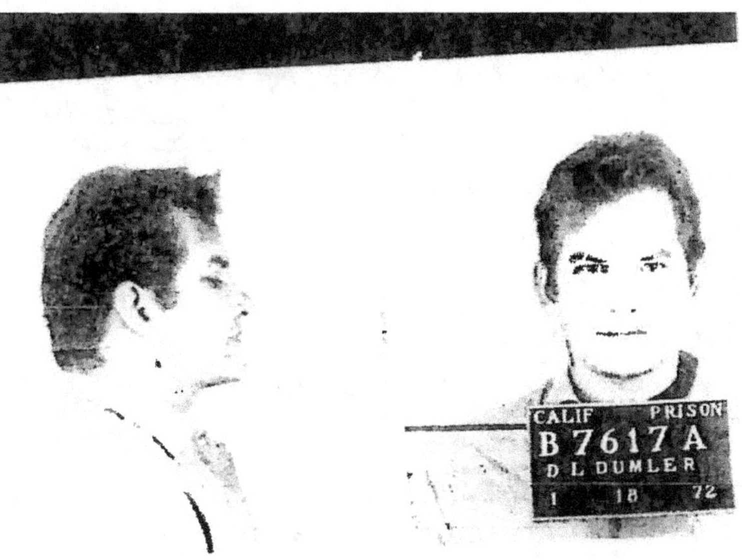

David Lee Dumler DOB: 1-7-33 At age 34 he was sentenced to five life sentences. 12-30-71 escaped from Folsom prison, captured same day, returned to San Quentin, discharged 3-10-77 at age 44. Had become an oil painter artist in prison. On 5-29-2002, he passed away at 69 from cardiorespiratory arrest!

"I am Glad I came your Way"

dedicated To: Evelyn Simms
Written by: Ben del Villar

A tribute to this lady
Who grew up with out frills
A humble start
but in her heart
the small things gave her thrills

She had a love for family
that none could change or sway
You would be blessed
like all the rest
If she had come your way

She loved the trees and flowers
and birds of every Kind,
so you might say
most everyday
hers were the "ties that bind".

Her task of raising children
was done with much devotion
she had no time
to fret or pine
she need not show emotion

Her task complete she moved out West
to live the "Golden Years"
Soon in her home
    she'd be alone
    and ponder why the tears

Her daughter urged her travel!
You'll see some of the World
too which she did
her emotions hid
her Adventure flag unfurled

through most of Northern Europe
with friend she ventured forth
to see the sights
as well as heights
and an occasional port

Her trips to see her children
became less frequent to be sure
soon health would fail
time would prevail
for this she had no 'cure

Now living with her daughter
her room dressed to her taste
she settled in
to sink or swim
time dictates; their's no haste

She's in God's hands, her life fullfilled
She knew she could not stay
she'd say don't cry
for you know I
am glad I came your way

2003 at mother's funeral the whole family was there! (In Carrollton, Missouri)

Mother passed Feb 16, 2003, at age 86!

Evelyn Rose Simms

2003

After mother had left us, Ben and I decided we should continue to fix the place in BHC and build a three car garage. The mobile we bought from Whitey and Jean we kept having trouble with the roof leaking so rather than put good money to bad we both said, "Let's just get a new one then we won't have that problem." That's what we did! After we got the new mobile everything had to be wired, also in the garage, bless his heart, Bob said, "Don't worry dad and mom I'll do all that for you" and he did he and Kerry came on weekends and holidays. Everything was very nice! We loved being able to go down there every chance we got!

2004

We made a couple of trips to see Ben and Suzy at their cabin in Big Bear. We got to see our two great grandsons Alan and Joshua. Ben and Suzy were host and hostess for the family reunion that year! They did a great job! We also made the trip when Nicki and Cain got married. Nicki was their youngest daughter. Our 47th anniversary was in May. I felt terrible because I had forgotten to buy Ben a card so I wrote one out on a piece of paper. (I did cook him a nice dinner, which he really enjoyed.) Ben also got a nice card from the boys and family on Father's Day! There were several times Ben would have to make a trip to the hide out without me so he could let the workers in the yard to do their work. He would write me a poem. Ben's handwriting was never that great (he always had secretaries to do his writing for him) but it was the words that mattered.

2005

This year I decided it would be a good idea for me to get a colonoscopy I never had one it was always advised to get one when you're 50. The outcome was not good and the doctors discovered I had a blockage in my intestines; long story short I ended up in the emergency room and the doctor removed 12 inches of my large intestine. The result was I ended up with a stoma bag which I still have. (17 years later) This year ended up being very busy. Since Ben was 77 and I was 70 we decided it was time we gave up the big house and the things that we needed to do to maintain the home were beginning to wear on our bodies.

Hardly anyone used the pool. (Not even Ben). The granddaughters were mostly married and were living elsewhere. We just felt (guess what?) Move On! Dan and Deena celebrated their 25th anniversary; their girls gave them a very nice party we were blessed with another great grandson, Blake (this was Sara and Ilan's) first child! Then another blessing great grandbaby Saveya was born she was Joey and Colleen's the first great-grandbaby girl! We were over joyed we were getting great grandbabies right and left! We went to visit our friend Kay in Camarillo, California and she took us to visit the Reagan library. It was really nice!

Two of Ben's sisters Enedina and Lola passed away. Ben wrote beautiful poems for each of them and later continued writing a poem for each brother and sister as they passed! Another family reunion was held in Big Bear, California. Finally our place in BHC Arizona was complete to our liking so now (you guessed it) it was time to look for our retirement home. We started looking everywhere we could think of that we might enjoy living. Lo and behold Boulder City here we come! We looked at this retirement home for 55 and up in Lake Mountain Estates! We both liked it a lot. It was a manufactured home; three bedrooms (this meant I wouldn't have a big house to clean) it was by the mountains and Lake Mead. We bought it and sold our big home. Believe me this is our last stop! Everyone off the train!

2006

With Bob and Kerry and friends Jim and Glenda, we got moved. We remodeled several areas of the mobile but settled in really nice! We celebrated our 49th. Ben gave me a card with another poem now we had BHC and because it was only 93 miles apart so we could go back-and-forth whenever we wanted to (which was about every two or three weeks) This was the year Ben Senior and Junior were in the Senior Olympics.

2007

Now was the year for our 50th. It was a total big surprise; our children planned a big celebration to be on the weekend of the family reunion in Phoenix. It was so wonderful we were so happy!

Bob, Kerry, and the girls came to BHC for Christmas, so Bob could do some electrical work in the garage. Bob did all our electrical work. He did an excellent job.

Bob and Ben Sr.

Christmas on the coffee table in BHC

This year's reunion was hosted by Ben and Suzy at their cabin in Big Bear. Ben Sr. and I got to see our great grandsons Alan and Joshua. They were so precious! There were our granddaughter Amy's sons. Joshua was 5, the 1st thing he said to us was, "Granddaddy, grandmother do you smoke?" We said, "Why would you ask that? No, Joshua we don't smoke." He said, "Oh good I don't want you to die." He had been told his Grandma Pat had died of cancer from smoking. This was the 2nd time we had come up to Ben and Suzy's cabin, we came in for Nicki's wedding before this.

Well here it was our 47th anniversary and I forgot to buy a card for Ben, so I wrote one out on a piece of paper!

5-25-04
J M.J.

To my husband - Happy 47th Anniversary!! You have brought so much comfort and joy into my life, and I cherish every moment we have had together. Like you say "Everyday is better than the day before" I love you with all my heart & soul. May we have many more years together and through eternity.

All my — Love & God you,

"Ma"

Nicki & Cain's wedding

Ben jr. Suzy Cain, Nichol granddaddy +

2004 Father's Day

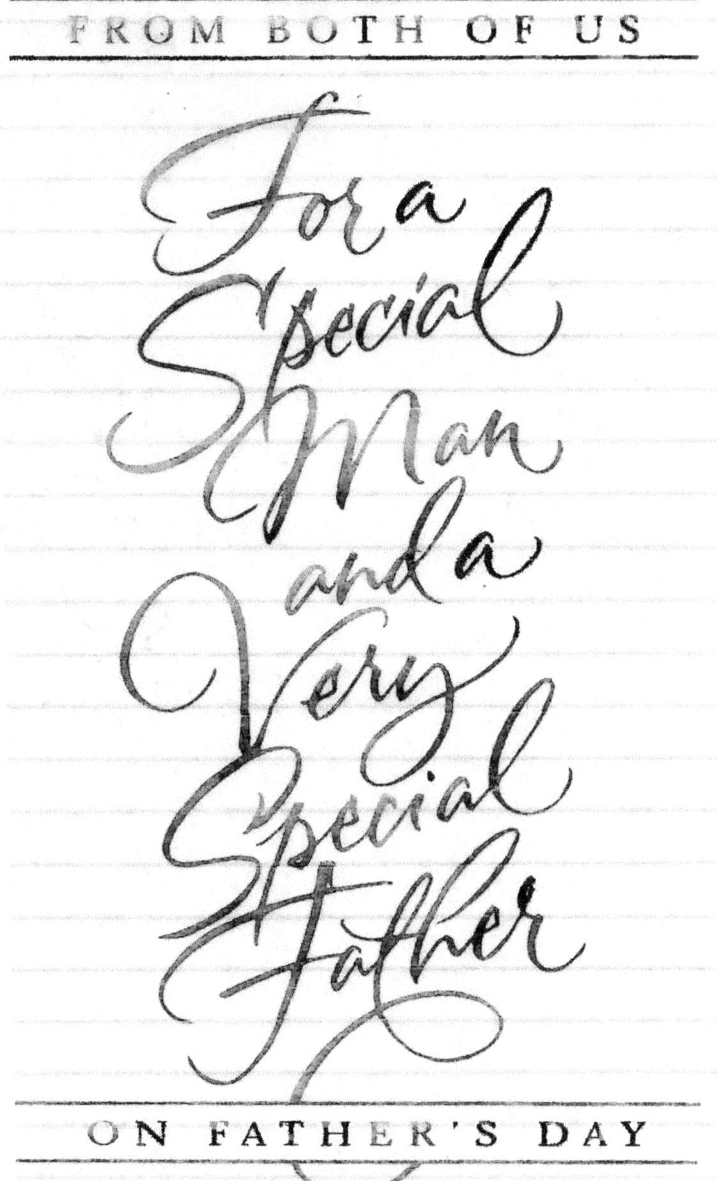

People in this day and age
don't always seem to care
About the special closeness
many families used to share,
But both of us are different,
and we find that, in our eyes,
There's nothing more important
than the bond of family ties...

That's why
you're on our minds so much
and always will be, too,
And why we hope you know
that we both think
the world of you.

His Chosen   9-8-04

I sit here in our "hideout" as workers ply their trade
Completing our garage inside, where a work bench will be made.
I must confess it's lonely, some what like lost in space
I hope they'll finish quickly, as I long to see your face.
With time To think, I do recall the many many years
I've shared with you through so much laughter, and occasionally tears.
We've done so much together, it's tough To be apart.
though space is now between us, you are with me in my heart
I am grateful To "my mother" who once looked at me + said ...
"of all the ladies you brought home, this one's so far ahead
her sage advice was heeded, and I'm so glad it was
you give me so much pleasure, and that is just because
your laughter, charm + full support, makes it all seem so dear
We've so much To be grateful for, our sons + their daughters Too;
all these things I think about, are mine because of you.
I write these words they're meant for you, they're meant for you alone,
for they convey the thoughts I have, the times when you are gone
were now in our declining years, but I am not afraid,
for if I left this world tomorrow, it easily could be said!
a gift from God had come his way, he did appreciate,
a fulfilled life of joy + love, with his chosen mate

Love always
Pa

There were times for some reason or another Ben and I would have to be apart. He would write me a poem.

G. M. G.   2-14-05

I loved you when first I saw you
the feeling got stronger with time
Fate pulled us apart a short while
But I felt one day you would   mine,
I choose to tell you   , how much I care for you
but words alone can not convey
the innermost thoughts I feel
or what I long to say.
So try to feel what this message says
As sure as the stars   shine
I wrote this little Sonnett
Just for you my Valentine

Love Always
Pa

2005

In and out of the 1st part of the year, our son Bob would drive from California to our place in Bullhead City, Arizona. He was hooking up all the electrical for us in the house and the garage and sheds. Bless his heart; he was so dedicated to help his dad and mom. While he worked on the electric, Ben contracted out to put the other side of our block wall, the sidewalks, driveways and install the fences on the front and back lots. Bob would work from the time he had breakfast until it was time to go to bed non-stop and it was plenty hot.

Bob would work from the time he had breakfast until time to go to bed. Non-stop and it was plenty hot.

This refrigerator was in the garage and dad would have a beer and Bob a soda pop. Bob he can't drink on the job.

The slab for the three car garage. Ben would get right in there and help whenever the workers would let him. Ben built nice work, benches in the garage and both sheds. As mother used to say, "He's handy as a pocket on a shirt."

For My Sweetheart

ON OUR ANNIVERSARY

I know I'm a lucky man
every time I look at you...
After all, how many men
have the joy of starting
and ending each day
by holding their sweetheart
in their arms?

How many men
get to go through life
with a woman by their side
who is as strong, capable, and intelligent
as she is beautiful,
inside and out?

How many men
know in their hearts
that they have the sweetest, most loyal,
most wonderful wife
in the whole wide world?

Me
5-25-06

(poem on back)

49 Years   5-25-06

These many years you've shared with me
Have swelled my heart & made it free
Though words alone can not convey
the inner feelings I try to say
show much I need you   By my side

I look upon you with certain pride
Knowing you're there no matter what
You always convey a pleasant thought
These words come to me from above —
Professing my ever increasing Love.

Yours
"Pa"

www.hallmark.com

U.S.A. 3.49
Canada 4.49
A 336-4
© HALLMARK LICENSING, INC.
HALLMARK CARDS, INC.
KANSAS CITY, MO 64141

Absolutely Stunning

426 Wedgewood Drive

Absolutely Pristine Condition Single Story Home on 1/3 Acre Lot • Bright, Open and Airy Floorplan with 2,303 Square Feet of Luxury Living Space • 3 Bedrooms and 3 Baths • Spacious Living Room • Large, Separate Family Room • Elegant Formal Dining Area • Bright, Cheery Kitchen with Breakfast Bar, Pantry, and Tile • Generous Master Suite with Walk-In Closet, and Private Bath with Double Sinks, Shower, and Separate Bathtub • Large Secondary Bedrooms with Mirrored Doors • Tons of Wonderful Extras Including: Intercom System, New AC Unit & Furnace, Berber Carpet, Ceramic Tile in Traffic Area, Solar Screens, Double-Sided Fireplace, Alarm System, Pot Shelves, Window Covers, and So Much More • Beautiful Backyard with Sparkling In Ground Pool, Detached Patio with Built-In BBQ Grill, 3-Hole Putting Green, and More • 3 Car Garage • Unbelievable Upgrades, Must See To Believe!

Offered At: $565,000

That night a senior group put on a show at UNLV.

The del Villars, father & son, compete in Senior Olympics

By Vince Addamo
Lovin' Life After 50

As the age expectancy of our population continues to rise, we are finding more and more father-son entrants into the Annual Nevada Senior Olympics.

This year 78-year-old Ben del Villar Sr. and his 54-year-old son, Ben Jr., will be competing for gold, silver and bronze medals. Ben Sr. has signed up for the high jump, racewalk and pistol shooting while Ben Jr. will be doing the hurdles, and high jump.

Both father and son have a long history of athleticism. Ben Sr. competed while in the Navy, running races while stationed at San Diego and also while on duty in China. After moving to Las Vegas in 1971 from Canoga Park, California, he continued with Corporate Challenge. He participated in the racewalk events while serving as casino executive for the Flamingo Hilton. He is celebrating his 49th wedding anniversary with his wife, Donna.

Ben Jr. attended Colorado State on a track scholarship. His major events are hurdles and high jump. In high school he ran for his school at the Mount SAC Relay. Ben Jr. lives in *Big Bear, California and is employed* by the Forest Service. He has been married to his wife Suzy for 35 years.

Other father-son entries have been 91-year-old James Pearce Sr. and his son James Jr., who competed together in the 2003 swimming events. Also, John and Michael Polish from Ely, Nevada, competed together for several years in golf and track & field. James Pearce Jr. had the added treat of watching his father, age 90 at the time, break the National Masters 50-meter freestyle record with a time of 40.4 seconds.

The 2006 Nevada Senior Olympics have their first events on September 23. This year there will be a greater opportunity for parent-child entries since a Masters Program has been added to include a 45-49 age category. Entrants in this category will have the same opportunity to earn medals, but are too young to be eligible to qualify for the National Senior Games in 2007. Applications can be obtained by calling 702-242-1590 or from the website, www.nevadaseniorolympics.com.

Ben Jr & Ben Sr.

115

2006 Senior Olympics- Dan and Deena and I went there to cheer Ben (dad) on.

This was the 1st ring he gave me (Emilee's birthstone)

There is a story about the design of the ring. I had a paper that was on a cigar that someone had left at our house and I liked the shape of it and wore it on my finger for several months. (I don't know why but I liked it! Then one day Ben came home and said "Here Ma throw that thing away. This is the real thing!"

A doll for each granddaughter that we gave to each one when they were twelve.

2014

Ben actually started umpiring and refereeing in California in 1969 and continued when we moved to Las Vegas. He was very active until 2014, Ben had said, "Ma when I can't keep up with those Jack rabbits then I'll hang it up." He bought a ceramic doll for all the granddaughters and gave me a ring for all their birthstones. The first ring he bought was his and my birthstone (sapphire his stone and diamonds my stone) this will go to Emilee.

1969 in CA

1974 Las Vegas

Sometimes Ben would travel to a nearby town

Las Vegas official "SNOA" (Southern Nevada Official Assn)

Hello Family and Friends,

We are very excited about the upcoming del Villar reunion in Arizona. The Vaught's have been busy making preparations and are hoping for a great turnout.

This year the reunion is very special as it will be Ben and Donna del Villar's 50th Wedding Anniversary. We are hoping that everyone will make special effort to attend and celebrate their 50 years of Love and Friendship.

We will be celebrating on Saturday evening and **IT IS A SURPRISE!** We will need everyone's efforts to keep the surprise from them and enjoy the weekend.

The family all ready has received some of the information in this letter. Friends however, have not.

Saturday – evening- May 26, 2007

Jeremie and Pamela will be hosting the **Celebration Dinner** at their home at 5:00 pm.

If you are unable to attend, we do understand, and would like to suggest that you might send a special message (photo, note, card) to Ben and Donna to let them know you are thinking of them. We know this would mean a great deal to Ben and Donna. **Please send any of these special wishes to Jeremie and Pamela Vaught's home as listed on the invitation. NOT BEN AND DONNA.**   Jeremie & Pamela Phone 480-539-2652

Please no Gifts!

For all of Ben and Donna's friends that are attending the Anniversary Dinner, we would like to invite you to our Family Reunion Picnic on Sunday. The information is as follows:

Sunday – May 27, 2007

10AM – The Reunion!!!! The reunion is going to be held at:

Shamrock Estates Neighborhood Park   .

The park is right down the street from Jeff and Leigh's house…

Just keep going straight on Rockwell.

This park should have something for everyone…basketball, volleyball, softball, and a playground. Get ready for some games!!! If it gets too hot, we can all head to Jeff and Leigh's for some A.C. and a dip in the pool, bring your suits!

Our sons and daughters-in-law pulled off a big surprise for Ben and me; they collected pictures (they found our wedding pictures) took them and I didn't even miss them. The family reunion just happened to be over the weekend of our 50th so it worked out perfectly. We were very surprised. It was so beautiful and touching to Ben's and my heart to think we were cared for by family and friends that much. That's another thing they took my Rolodex so they could get names and addresses for people to contact; again they were sneaky. They had very nice invitations printed up.

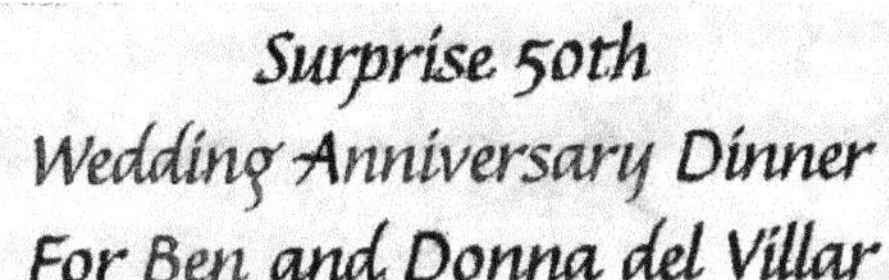

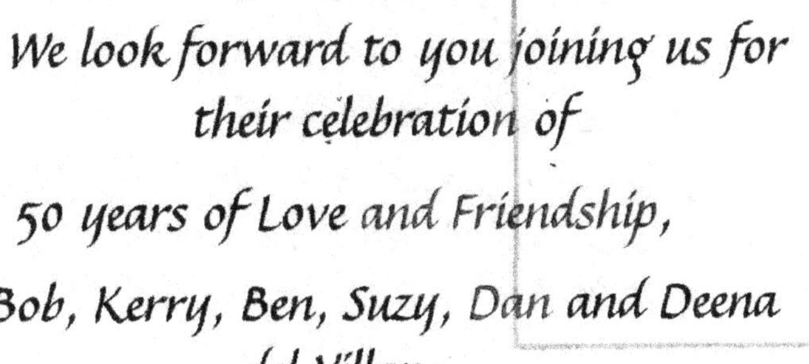

Mr. and Mrs. del Villar
Happy 50th Anniversary!

Ben and Donna del Villar were pleasantly surprised at their 50th Wedding Anniversary held in Gilbert, AZ, (Pheonix), at the home of Jeff and Leigh Ann Vaught (grand nephew and niece). It was planned by their three sons and their wives: Robert and Kerry, Ben L. Jr. and Suzy, also Daniel and Nadine del Villar. The gathering was held in conjunction with the annual del Villar family reunion, with 82 people in attendance. Ben Sr., a retired Casino Executive, and Donna, a retired Accounting Supervisor, who now live in Boulder City, were completely taken off guard, and thoroughly enjoyed the company of their children, grandchildren, and great grandchildren, as well as family and friends.

GHT Newsletter *this was in the "Knights of Columbus Newsletter"* Page 4

"50th WEDDING ANNIVERSARY"
May 25, 2007

Sir Knight Ben & Donna del Villar attended a yearly Family Reunion in Gilbert Arizona, with offspring's son Robert & wife Kerry, son Ben L. JR. & wife Suzi, and son Dan & wife Deena. To their surprise… they were given a 50th Wedding Anniversary Party.

Congratulations!!

MOM & DAD
50TH WEDDING ANNIVERSARY
WE LOVE YOU BOTH
THANK YOU FOR BEING OUR
MOM AND DAD, AND ALWAYS
BEING THERE FOR OUR FAMILIES

✱ This was from our oldest son, Bob, he would always let us know how much he loved us!

This was in the Knights of Columbus newsletter.

Ma

Why is it that sometimes
your arms are the only place
where I can find peace?
Just a smile from you,
and all the problems of the world
suddenly seem unimportant.

Why is it that even when life
isn't perfect, I know that
as long as we're in it together,
things will always turn out okay?
Just having you by my side
makes each day happier and brighter.

Why is it that out of all
the millions of people in the world,
I was lucky enough to find
the one person who was meant to be
my lifetime love?

Maybe some things
aren't meant to be questioned,
only cherished.
Like I cherish you.

5 15 01
J. m. J.

For the
Woman
I Love

ON OUR
ANNIVERSARY

It doesn't say it all
but you know
Love always
A

(over)

FOR NOW & EVER MORE   7-11-07
                                        1:30 pm

We're married now for 50 years, I've known you 53
When first we met, my eyes were wide, yet then I did not see,
how truly blessed my future was, you'd soon be at my side,
I now reflect, recall the years, with certain inner pride,
each and every day I've told you, since we made our vows together,
how much your loved and cared for, but I can not be sure whether,
my words are adequate for what I really try to say,
but I'll still tell you daily, in every truthful way.
I wait for you impatiently, not knowing what's in store,
gratful for the years we've had, and wish for many more.
Appreciating blessed gifts, Sun, stars, Moon even skies
but they can't replace my feelings, when I look into your eyes.
Wife and mother, best of friend, you're all these things & more,
How can I put it into words, your one I can't ignore
Try as I may to think of ways to express my thoughts for you,
nothing seems appropriate, no words can say what's true.
With these lines I try to say, and let you know for sure
My feelings for you are sincere, also deep & Pure.
As the desert sand keep drifting and the sea returns to shore
you can be sure I'm here for you, for now & evermore

                    Love always
                        Pa

2008

Ben bought his last bike, a Harley Street Glide. He said, "I'm so proud Ma that you like to ride with me; we're a team! But I think it's time to hang it up." Ben was 80 the color of the Harley was atomic orange and we had matching helmets. (he sold the Harley in 2013 after we moved to Boulder City.

Ben lost his beloved sister Van (short for Evangelina) she was one year older than Ben. Growing up they were almost inseparable! In later years they taught each other to dance. Van's job was to wash the dishes. Ben turned out to be a wonderful dancer. That's one of the reasons he was so popular in college. As he did for all his brothers and sisters who went before him Ben wrote their eulogy and a poem about them. We had our first snow in Boulder City it was a real surprise they had to close the airport as they did not have the machinery to clear the snow.

The mountains around us were beautiful. It snowed on Christmas morning (who could ask for anything better). After 51 years we had a little snow on our roof too! Ha! Our place in Bullhead was just about a half hour from Oatman, Arizona, which was an old mining town off Highway 66. There were donkeys in the streets; it was very historical I took a picture of Ben standing sideways with his stomach sticking out. I said, "Are you pregnant?" He said, "Oh I'm just carrying it for a friend."

2009

After we did all the upgrades to Boulder City and Bullhead City, we had a gigantic garage sale in our three car garage (BHC). We had some good friends from Tucson, Arizona (Paul and Nancy one of Ben's college buddies and his wife) came for Thanksgiving. Ben always liked to pull tricks on Paul so Ben said, 'Ma I want you to cook up a capon chicken (they are very small) then when we sit down to dinner I'll hold my carving knife and you take the lid off of the plate and there will be the capon. I want to see the look on Paul's face I'll have reservations then we will take them out to dinner." We did just that it was very funny!

2010

We made a trip to Tucson Arizona to pay back the visit with Paul and Nancy; they took us to the Gaslight Theater where you had to dress up old time. A guy played the piano to match the movie that was showing. We were served popcorn and beer and it was lots of fun!

2011

My sister Denise from Texas came to visit. We took her to the hideout and out to dinner in the gourmet restaurant at the Riverside Hotel in Laughlin.

2012

Ben and I rented tables and chairs then set up Christmas in our garage in BHC. We had our sons and all their families and we had made albums of Ben's family history all the way back to Spain. They were really nice albums. Everyone was very happy to see them. Then we exchanged gifts and now it was time for entertainment. Ben brought out his entertainment; the boombass he had a record he played while he kept time with the music; it was a snappy tune. Everyone had a blast trying to play it.

2013

We had a big celebration for Father's Day then again on Ben's 85th birthday.

2014

I forgot to mention we had a Corvette since 2005 then in 2008 we got our second Corvette; it was mahogany red. We had joined the Corvette Club also in 2005; it was Ben's dream car but this year 2014 the time came we were both having trouble getting in and out of it so Ben said, "As much as I hate it I might as well admit it I'm too old for this car." I said, "Whatever you decide is okay with me."

In 2015, we went on a few Corvette rallies plus one regular family reunion but in October Ben traded the Corvette in on a 2016 Escalade Cadillac. After the trade in, the Cadillac was $80,000 and we paid cash. Ben said, "Ma did you ever think 58 years ago when we first started out that we would ever be able to do this?" I said, "Not in a million years."

In 2016 our son Bob had retired after 40 years in the electrical trade. Since Bob had always been what you might call a work and no play person to speak of because his only interest was to provide for his wife Kerry and his girls and anyone who needed his help. He got a check up and came to find out he had cancer in one kidney; after that his mental state became very distant because he would sit and stare out the window for hours at a time. He would not take his medication as prescribed by the doctors. The family took him to several different doctors he was becoming more and more aloof to everyone and in a deep depression.

EVANGELINA

Remember this great lady, as we know should
As God designed his angels, she was everything that's good
She dearly loved her father, they were close as they could be
Too young to understand why he died so suddenly
She quickly learned her duties, took little brother by the hand,
Together they began their schooling, much too young to understand
Their age difference, demanded she move on ahead
By now he had adapted, no more tears would either shed
The years flew by and she matured, her talents she displayed,
A promising young artist, many paintings she had made
Three older brothers off to the war, and two others soon to go
She worked to help the household budget, if for nothing else to show
That she would do her part to help both family and home
Completing her education, there was no desire to roam
Soon she would meet and date the one who stood out from the rest
A blue eyed blonde, a dancer too, he would survive the test
They married soon and kept their vows through good times, and in bad
And anyone who knew them were very, very glad
To be part with this happy couple, whom would soon start family
Four lovely children came to be, she cherished happily
With un-matched patience, she would show her love and understanding
Hearing stories, fixing "boo-boo's", she brought a happy ending
Admired and respected by people near and far
She stood out as no other much like the morning star
She leaves us now, her task is done, now resting peacefully
You must know she is watching, from a place most heavenly
The joy she brought like music from a well played concertina
We are so lucky to have had our own Evangelina

DOB: 04/28/1927   DOD: 02/14/2008
Prepared by Ben L del Villar 02/17/2008

While we were at the hide out at BHC one weekend, we decided to take a side trip to Oatman, Arizona which is only about ½ hour drive. It is an old mining town by the original Highway 66 and they have donkeys that roam the streets. Ben forgot his cowboy hat! That's why he has the disgusted look! Also he doesn't have his horse will tell you about his cowboy days later. Darlene is my cousin and part of the cowboy history later!

After 51 years we had a little snow on our roof too!

Ben got his tan leather motorcycle outfit.
He didn't care if there was snow on the ground or on the roof.

2009 April

We were finished with all the upgrades we did to the mobile and the three car garage was full of things we didn't need or want anymore; time for a garage sale! Everyone who helped us they could have one item anything of their choice before the sale began and believe me it was a lot of work. we could not have done it without them We made close to $4000- not bad –tax free ha!

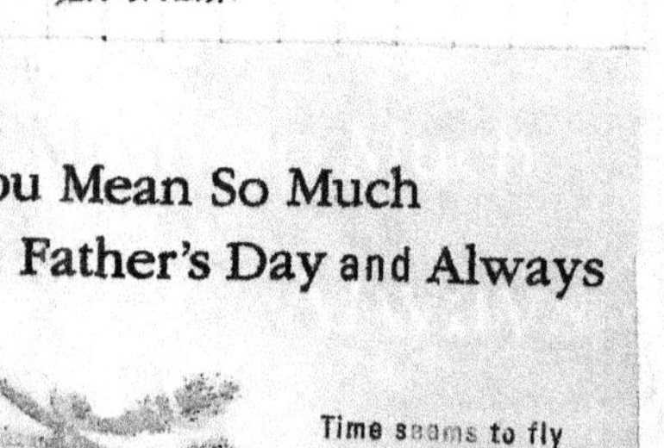

Ben loved all his babies, and they loved him!

You Mean So Much
on Father's Day and Always

Time seems to fly

in this busy world —

and our warm thoughts

of the special people

in our lives

too often go unspoken,

even though the feelings

are always in our hearts...

That's why Father's Day

is a perfect chance

to remind you

of some important things

that are true all year...

...how much you mean,

how special you are,

and how warmly

you're wished

every happiness.

6-16-13

Happy Father's Day

Granddaddy,

We love you so much! You have not only been a great example as a father but also as a granddaddy & great granddaddy. We love you and hope you have a great day. ♡ Timmy, Emilee & Matthew

It's having someone who can make
your heart skip a beat
with just a smile.
Someone you can always count on,
no matter what.
Someone who loves you
just for being "you."

Lucky me, I found
my perfect someone
when I found you.

Happy Birthday

Dear Ben ~
you are my love forever & ever!
Everyday our love gets stronger
Have a great fun day with
your honey! ME, OF COURSE !!
Love & God bless you!
"MA."

9-24-13
J.M.J.
Ben's 85th B/D

My sister "Denise" in Laughlin NV 2011

2012 X-mas in BHC garage

April Ben and Donna 2014

We had a corvette for several years and belonged to the Corvette Club. It was Ben's dream car until the time came when we were both having trouble getting in and out of it! Story later!

2017

In March we had a catastrophic tragedy Bob took his own life! All the family was devastated! Why was the big question! It took me months to come to grips with what had happened to our wonderful, loving son. I finally decided he didn't do what he did because he didn't love us. He did what he did because he does love all his family he felt like he had become a burden and he didn't want to be a burden to anyone.

Ben Senior never did get over it, I would find him alone at times sobbing about Bob. (It wasn't like Ben to cry) Bob's funeral was the best (Kerry made sure of that) it was amazing to see how many people were at the funeral over 200 (Ben wrote a poem for Bob called My Son! Dan read it at the funeral) and then many came up to Ben and me to tell us how Bob had in some way touched their lives.

It was shortly after that Ben Senior started being ill. He developed a terrible itch. After a biopsy it was determined his third layer of skin had edema. I felt so bad for him and he would itch all day and all night; he never complained the doctor had him on several pills, steroids, finally the doctor wanted him to get Dupixent shots once a month which after about a year were starting to help his itching

December was our sixtieth year together for Christmas our family still had heavy hearts. (it wasn't the same without Bob either being with us or calling!) Ben and I would sometimes say, I wonder why God never allowed us to have a biological child then would say, "He just wanted us to love and take care of the ones we already had, premade!" For some reason I never got pregnant (it wasn't from lack of trying our sex life was always the greatest.)

2018

Ben's health continued to go downhill; he had an enlarged prostate which caused him to lose control of his bladder, and the result was he had ended up with a bag. Bless his heart he tried so hard to be strong but would lose his balance and fall. Many times I would have to call 911. The fellows would come and help him get up! I had bought him a walker the fellows from the fire department put it together for me.

At first with my help Ben could get out of bed or a chair. He needed help with everything! Probably 80% of my day was spent helping him. He would tell me every day how much he loved me and thanked me for helping him, I said, "You would do the same for me." He said, "I sure would." We started calling ourselves the Lee twins ugly and beastly but we could not decide which was which! Because we both had a bag!

2019

Even though Ben's health was not good, I wanted to do something special for his 90th birthday! With Dan and Deena's help we went on a cruise from St. Louis to Nashville where we went to the Grand Old Opry. Ben enjoyed getting to go but without Dan and Deena's help we could not have made the trip. Ben had always been so active it was very degrading for him to be so helpless. Still he was not a complainer. Ben received many get well cards; he would say, "Ma I love my wonderful family! I would tell him, "They love you, too!" At the family reunion Ben gave his gun collection to his son's brother, nephews and son-in-laws; he knew he would not ever be able to use them again

San Fernando Mission Cemeteries and Mission Hills Catholic Mortuary

---

Robert Lee del Villar

(October 15, 1951 - March 03, 2017)

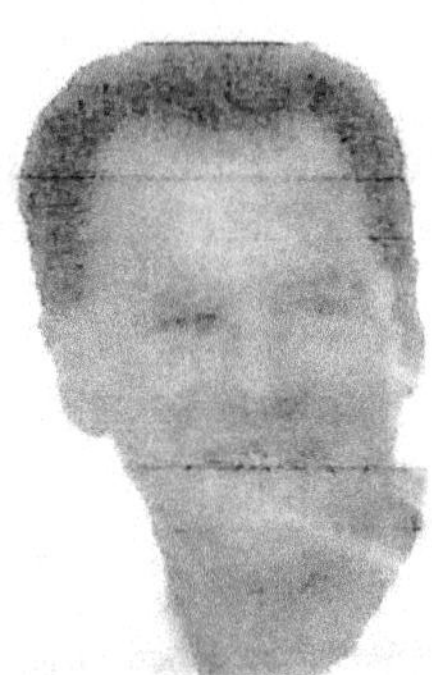

Robert Lee del Villar was born on October 15, 1951 in Kansas City, Missouri. He grew up in the San Fernando Valley with his mother Donna, father Benjamin, and his brothers Dan and Ben Jr.

As a young boy, he loved sports like baseball, basketball, water & snow skiing and he was exceptionally good at all of them. He was a boy scout and he loved camping. He graduated from Cleveland High School in 1969, but not before he met the love of his life, Kerry Ann Corcoran, in Spanish class. He must have been enamored because he never did learn to speak a bit of Spanish. Shortly after her graduation, Bob and Kerry were married on June 12, 1971.

They worked hard as a young wed couple, working at a gas station and Gemco until Bob decided on trade school for his career. In 1974 he began working for IBEW Local 11. It was the electrical trade that he loved and he did well for more than forty years. He was hardworking and the kind of man who never called in sick. He woke up before the sunrise each morning to provide for his family. It didn't matter if the job was installing the lights of the LA Convention Center, The Hollywood Bowl, A high rise somewhere, The B2 Bomber hanger, or just in a neighbor's living room, the job was always done in a meticulous, professional fashion that only Bobby "Hi-Tech" could do.

After having four adoring daughters, Bob and Kerry moved to Saugus, California in 1983. It was there the "house" became a home...living in Saugus for more than thirty years; raising their girls. During those years, Bob coached many years of his girls' softball teams and hosted numerous golf tournaments for HART baseball league. The baseball field became a home away from home. Many close friends were made during those years...friendships Bob always held near and dear to his heart. He was also a helpful member in his community as a member of the Lions Club

144

for several years. Bob always loved to be a helper in any fashion, and he especially loved to help friends in need.

Bob loved a good routine and he was an outdoors kinda guy. Every summer, just like clockwork he packed up and headed out to Lake Mead with his parents, his brother's family, his wife, his kids and his best friends. During those trips, he loved the water, the sunshine, the laughter, the country music and to drive his kids in a boat much faster than Kerry approved of. He taught all four of his daughters to water ski and probably a good 25 of their friends over the years. It was what he loved. He loved to share what he knew and what he was proud of with others. He was a simple man, but could chat with anyone and everyone he met about anything. He was so friendly and charismatic with his great big smile and silly laugh. He got a kick out of making his girls laugh with his wiggle dances he would do; and as most know, he never missed a chance to tell a good joke. One of the most important times of the year for him was the del Villar Family reunion...he absolutely loved catching up with his aunts, uncles and cousins. He loved the laughs, the stories, and just being around family.

Bob's girls were his absolute pride and joy. He felt accomplished being able to give each of them an education. When the time came for each of them to marry their loves you could see his glow as he walked them down the aisle to their new lives. Bob grew to love the four sons he never knew he wanted; and he especially loved the nine grandchildren that were brought into his life. He loved and adored each of his grandbabies with all his heart.

Every one of his girls, sons, and grandchildren adored him, and will remember him for many different reasons and special moments but mostly for being kind, eager, generous, loyal, loving, responsible, and so funny.

As Kerry will always say...Robert Lee was the most sincere, gentle soul any of us ever knew. He was the most hardworking, dedicated, generous, loving man any wife or daughter could hope for. He is the love of her life. He will be missed immeasurably. Rest In Peace Pop-Pop. May God hold your beautiful soul.

A Funeral Service will be held on Friday March 31, 2017 at Mission Hills Mortuary in the Mortuary Chapel.
Burial will follow at San Fernando Mission Cemetery.
There will be a Reception at the home of Karnel and Greg Watkins.

"My Son"

There is so much to tell about this great and loving man
We cannot know the destiny, within our ~~Saviors~~ plan
When just a child, within his room he'd cover up his head
Quick to notice we would see, there was something he would dread
Upon our asking why? then he was very quick to say:
"because I don't like whiskers", but he would get them anyway
As he got older, he soon learned, I wasn't all that bad
UCLA season tickets for football, a sport which made him glad
Two tickets were for travel games, one at Stanford one at Cal
In the hotel in San Francisco he said "Dad you are my pal"
Boxing matches once a week, to learn of self defense
The thought was to instill in him the things that made most sense
He grew up way to quickly, a dedicated family man
A love of wife and children was always in his plan
His sense of humor would come forth, with his infectious smile
He'd lead into his story, with words that would beguile
A father, friend and counselor, he left us way to soon.
My deepest feelings would come forth, when he'd ... walk into the room
We'd engage in conversations, and it would be no surprise,
when looking at his face, I'd see he had his mother's eyes
With heavy heart I realize his race is finally done,
As is with his two brothers, he will always be my son.

Written by Father
Ben L. del Villar Sr.
10/15/51 - 3/3/17

2018

9-24-28

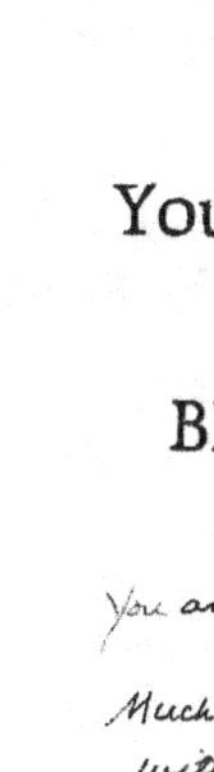

...because
You were born!

HAPPY
BIRTHDAY!

You are my sunshine!

Much love + God bless you,
with many more happy
birthdays.

As Always ~ 'Ma'

Especially For You
On Your

90th

Birthday

9-24-2018

Granddaddy,

No wonder you have
all of our love
and good wishes today.

You are truly an amazing man! We love that you keep having your fun, incredible adventures at this time in your life! You are an inspiration to us all! We love you very much! Happy 90th DoooDaddy!
Love + God Bless You!
Tim + Erin

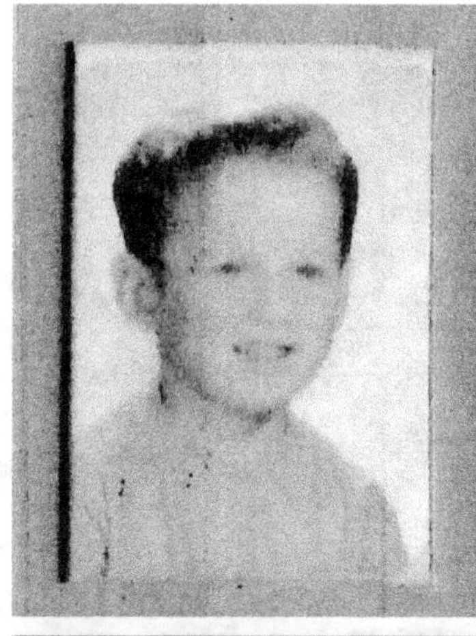

*Bob, born
October 15, 1951*

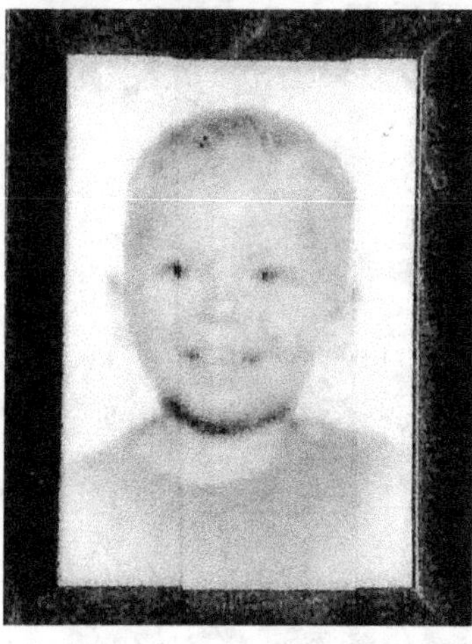

*Ben Jr., born
March 24, 1952*

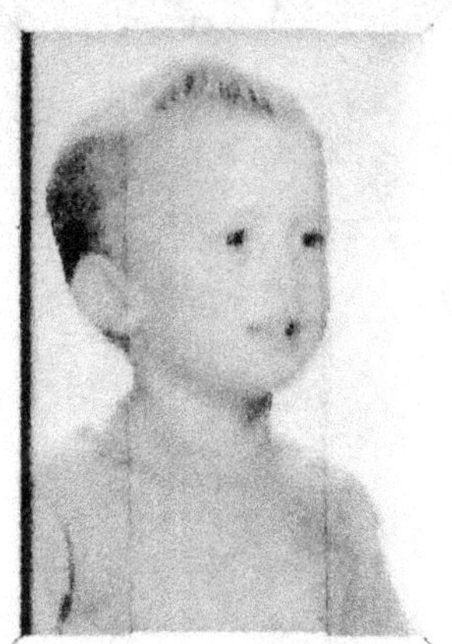

*Dan, born
October 31, 1953*

Ben and I could never get over how much they resembled each other.

Cumberland River

Travel the scenic Cumberland River from Nashville to St. Louis on this 8-day voyage. Enjoy stops along the way including Clarksville, Dover, Paducah, Cape Girardeau, and Chester. Cruise past rocky cliffs and through national forests. Visit the Grand Ole Opry in Nashville. Witness the migratory songbirds, woodpeckers, and red-tailed hawks that make the river come alive in this exciting route of adventure and intriguing history.

Our cruise was very nice. Dan and Deena went with Ben and I so they could help the two old people.

Being a cowboy, Ben really enjoyed the Grand Ole Opry.

2019

Ben had a beautiful gun and rifle collection but he decided he wanted to give almost all of them away to his sons, nephews, and grandson-in-laws at the 2019 family reunion. He had bought those with the dollars he earned from the umpiring and refereeing as he did when he bought me all those rings.

Christmas is happiness,
Christmas is enchantment,
Christmas is special—
because of people like you.

Sending love and hugs to you
both always.

Merry Christmas!

✻ Digital Photo Frame

Dec 2019

This is a special gift full of love for the two
of you to enjoy. It is pre-loaded with many
special pictures of all of your babies for you
both to enjoy. All you need to do is plug it in,
sit back, and enjoy your beautiful family
We love you both so very much.

Love and God bless,

Kerry, The Stanleys, The Diazs, The Bouzaglos
and The Thorntons

Nov 2020

Granddaddy,

Hope you are feeling better in no time.
Get Well Soon!

We love you so much and hope
you feel better with each new day.
We miss you and hope to see you
soon!
♡ Timmy, Emilee, Matthew,
Lillee and Jayde

The Broken Chain

We little knew that morning that
God was going to call your name.
In life we loved you dearly, in death
we do the same. It broke our
hearts to lose you, you did not go
alone; for part of us went with you,
the day God called you home. You
left us peaceful memories, your love
is still our guide; and though we
cannot see you, you are always at our
side. Our family chain is broken,
and nothing seems the same;
but as God calls us one by one,
the Chain will link again.

2020

"By now Ben could not hardly sit up without help. Dan (bless his heart), came to be with us to help lift Dad out of the bed and etc. Ben was having mini strokes that affected his speech. It became obvious to Dan and I, Ben needed 24 hour care so we called hospice. I had to feed him non-solid foods, because it was very hard for Ben to swallow! On Dec 6, 2020, hospice brought an adjustable bed. The fire department guys came and put Ben in the bed! We had Father Zanoni from church come and give Ben his last rites. Ben said to me, "Ma, why doesn't God just take me. I'm not good for you, or anyone." I told him, "If that's what you really what, I'll ask God if he can do that." Ben left us that night around 2:00 a.m. Dec 7, Pearl Harbor Day! I forgot, after Father Zanoni left on the morning of Dec 6 Ben told Dan how much he loved him and he thanked Dan for being there to help his dad! Very touching, it brought tears to my eyes.

Dan was a blessing; he contacted everyone made arrangements for Ben's mass and funeral services at the Veteran's Memorial Cemetery. The service was on January 7, 2021.

2020

December 7 has been a sad day since it is Pearl Harbor Day but now it is an even sadder day for me and my family. It was the day my husband Ben after 63 years was called home to be with God! I loved him so much and always will! He was a wonderful husband, father, granddad, and friend. I said hopefully he can see Bob again also his mother, dad, and all his family that went before him. I said a little prayer to help me accept what had happened.

God Grant me the strength to except the things I cannot change the courage to change the things I can and the wisdom to know the difference

Dear God, I want to take a minute not to ask for anything from you but to simply thank you for all I have and had!

To me this is what Ben lived by, faith hope and love!
Life is not a race but indeed a journey, be honest, work hard, be choosy
Say thank you, I love you and great job to someone each day
Go to church, take time for prayer, the Lord giveth and the Lord taketh
Let your handshake mean more than pen and paper
Love your life and what you've been given it is not accidental
Search for your purpose and do it as best you can
dreaming does matter it allows you to become that which you inspire to
Laugh often appreciate the little things in life and enjoy them
Some of the best things really are free
Do not worry less wrinkles are more becoming
Forgive it frees the soul
Take time for yourself plan for longevity
Recognize the special people you've been blessed to know
Live for today enjoy the moment.
This is my message, "In the end I know God loves me, because he blessed me
with the best"

2021

It was a long and lonesome year but I had so many wonderful cards and phone calls from family and friends (Dan has called me every night, what a blessing). My neighbors have been so caring no doubt my life will never be the same but I will always be grateful for what I have and have had!

2022

I don't know what the future holds for me but I hope I can stay safe and well for a few more years and I hope when God calls me home I will see Ben and Bob once again! In the end I'm so grateful to God for giving me such a wonderful family, a loving husband, so many kind lifelong friends, three sons, three daughters-in-law, nine granddaughters, thirteen great grandbabies, one great great granddaughter, and wonderful neighbors, who could ask for more! That's my life!

This came from the 2012 family album we gave to the members of our family that year.

Mr. & Mrs. Ben Del Villar

"Year 2000"

this was our last
lake trip

We have a lot of
fond memories

of so many fun times

Love + God bless you,

Grandaddy + Grandmother

Our 3 sons and
their beautiful
families   —>

Bob, Kerry, Erin, Colleen, Sara, and Emilee

Ben Jr., Suzy, Amy, and Nicki

Dan, Deena, Louisa, Elena, Mary

WE THE DELVILLAR DESCENDANTS ARE ONCE AGAIN BLESSED FOR SEVEN MORE GENERATIONS. THE ODDS OF US GETTING THIS CLOSE TO THE HOLY FATHER WERE EXTREME, BUT OUR PRAYERS WERE ANSWERED. THE FAMILY LAST RECEIVED THE PAPAL BLESSING BETWEEN 1750 AND 1760. (MAMA THOUGHT IT WAS 1752) WE ARE NOW COVERED TO 2151 I HAD NO IDEA WHAT WAS INVOLVED WHEN I MADE THE PROMISE; (HARDLY MORE THAN A CHILD) HOWEVER, WITH ELEVEN BROTHERS AND SISTERS BEHIND ME, WE HAD TO BE SUCCESSFUL. HOPEFULLY A SUCCESSOR WILL KNOW OF THIS IN 168 YEARS, AND CONTINUE THE PILGRIMAGE. HE/SHE WOULD HAVE TO HAVE THE STRENGTH AND COURAGE TO REMAIN BASICALLY TRUE TO THE HOLY MOTHER CHURCH, AS THE DELVILLAR WOMEN HAVE. HAD THIS NOT BEEN A SPECIAL HOLY YEAR, THE GRANTING OF SPECIAL REQUESTS WOULD NOT HAVE BEEN EXTENDED. OUR REQUEST WAS MADE TO AND GRANTED BY POPE JOHN PAUL 2ND 11:30 AM OCTOBER 5TH 1983.

YOUR LOVING BROTHER:
DONNA TOD.

Ben, was a man with many skills + interests. We never had To hire an electrican + very seldom a plummer, or carpenter. He was always able to read directions very well.

Ben, was a man who loved "God", family, + his country. He was a good son, husband father, Granddaddy, Brother, Uncle, + friend To all. He never let anyone down! He did Kinda go overboard when it came to clothes, Motorcycles, guns, cars, but what the hell, as he would say "if it aint broke don't fix it".

Ben, was a very special person to me, and all that Knew him!

It was a wonderful life, with my catch of a lifetime!

I will always be convinced that it was fate that brought us together + I thank "God" everyday, he gave us that chance!!

Rest in peace, your forever in my heart!

I Love You,

"MA"

Benjamin (Ben) del Villar
September 24, 1928 - December 7, 2020

God Looked around His garden
and found an empty place.

He then looked down upon the
earth and saw your tired face.

He put His arms around you
and lifted you to rest.

God's garden must be beautiful;
He always takes the best.

He saw the road was getting rough,
and the hills were hard to climb,
so He closed your weary eyelids
and whispered "Peace be thine."

It broke our hearts to lose you,
but you didn't go alone,
for part of us went with you
the day God called you home.

In Loving Memory of
Benjamín
del Villar
Sept. 24, 1928 ~ Dec 7, 2020
May you live in peace this
day, may your home be
with God in Zion, with
Mary, the virgin Mother of
God, with Joseph, and all the
angels and saints.

May you return to your
Creator, who formed you
from the dust of the earth.
May holy Mary, the angels,
and all the saints come to
meet you as you go forth
from this life. May you see
your Redeemer face to face.

Safely Home

I am home in Heaven, dear ones;
  Oh, so happy and so bright!
There is perfect joy and beauty
  In this everlasting light.

All the pain and grief is over,
  Every restless tossing passed;
I am now at peace forever,
  Safely home in Heaven at last.

Did you wonder I so calmly
  Trod the valley of the shade?
Oh! but Jesus' love illumined
  Every dark and fearful glade.

And He came Himself to meet me
  In that way so hard to tread;
And with Jesus' arm to lean on,
  Could I have one doubt or dread?

Then you must not grieve so sorely,
  For I love you dearly still;
Try to look beyond earth's shadows,
  Pray to trust our Father's will.

There is work still waiting for you,
  So you must not idly stand;
Do it now, while life remaineth —
  You shall rest in Jesus' land.

When that work is all completed,
  He will gently call you home;
Oh, the rapture of that meeting,
  Oh, the joy to see you come!

FORGET-ME-NOT
Cynoglossum Blue

When I come to the end of the road,
  And the sun has set for me,
I want no rites in gloom-filled rooms.
  Why cry for a soul set free?

Miss me a little, but not too long,
  And not with your head bowed low;
Remember the love that we once shared...
  Miss me, but let me go!

For this is a journey that we all must take,
  And each must go alone.
It's all a part of the Master's plan
  A step on the road to home.

When you are lonely and sick of heart,
  Go to the friends we know,
And busy your sorrows in doing good deeds.
  Miss me but let me go

Feb 2021

Aunt Donna,

Asking God to enfold you
in His faithful love and comfort you
with the cherished memories
you hold dear.

We are so sorry for the loss of Uncle Ben. He was a very special person! And the "Rock" of our Family (You Too!) He will always be in our thoughts & Prayers

God Bless —
Love always Tim & Tami

Let us encourage one another...
Hebrews ~~10:25~~
10:24

Our Prayer:
When you close your eyes for the last time in
this world, and open them again in the next,
the first face you will see is the face of Jesus.
With His arms stretched out to you,
and a smile on His face, saying,
"Job well done, my son."   "Welcome Home."

What a blessed life, a legacy and example
you will leave for us to follow.

...to cheer you.

With Love
Tinker & Alice

Xmas - 2021

2021

... For another banquet table
abounds with joy and love,
For those who've made the journey
to be with our Lord above.

This season, may you celebrate
the Faith that is the heart of Christmas,
the Hope that lies ahead in heaven,
and the Love of those we hold in our arms
and in our memories.

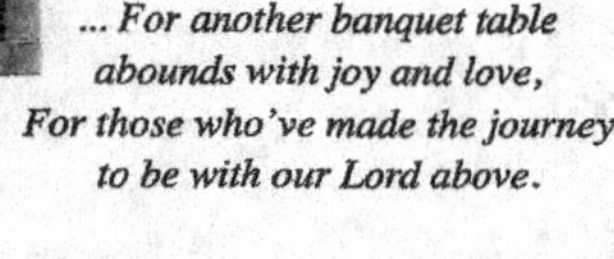

Looking back I have so much
To be grateful for, and looking
forward I am thankful To be
blessed with family and
friends like you!
Love + God Bless you ~ Donna

From: Ben To "Ma"